STeven

COARSE FISHING

Warner

D0620707

Pan Anglers' Library

COARSE FISHING

Edited by
Kenneth Mansfield

PAN BOOKS LTD
LONDON AND SYDNEY

First published 1972 by Barrie & Jenkins Ltd.
This edition published 1973 by Pan Books Ltd,
Cavaye Place, London SW10 9PG

ISBN 0 330 23510 9

2nd Printing 1974

© Barrie & Jenkins Ltd 1972

*Made and printed in Great Britain by
Cox & Wyman Ltd, London, Reading and Fakenham*

CONTENTS

INTRODUCTION

This book brings together, in whole or in part, several titles from the well-known 'How to Catch Them' series. They have been brought up-to-date and, together with a considerable amount of new material have been welded into a comprehensive handbook on coarse fishing.

After some preliminary remarks on law and licences, there are full sections on tackle, and on baits and groundbait. These – and the next section, on roach, which deals at length with the techniques of float fishing, ledgering and long–trotting – give most of the required general information on coarse fishing. Therefore the succeeding sections, dealing with fish other than roach, do not repeat matters already described, but refer only to tackles and techniques peculiar to the species under discussion.

K.M.

J. G. ROBERTS

Coarse Fishing

The origin of the word 'coarse' as applied to fish is un-traceable. It is an unfortunate word, but one that is here to stay. There is no such thing in law. Acts governing inland fisheries refer to salmon, trout, char and eels by their names. All the remaining freshwater fish are called just that – 'fresh-water fish'. Excluded from the group are those fish that mi-grate to and from salt water – shad, for example.

From the angler's point of view the important species of coarse fish in the British Isles are barbel, common bream, common carp, crucian carp, chub, dace, perch, pike, roach, rudd and tench. To these can be added eels (which do not spawn in fresh water); three types of pike-perch (American, European and zander) – which need scientific examination for identification and are therefore best called by the angler 'pike-perch', without frills; some small fish, of which gud-geon, bleak and ruffe reach recorded weight status; and sea-going species like the lamprey.

We are here concerned only with the species that the angler sets out to catch.

ENGLAND AND WALES

There is a statutory close season for coarse fish extending from March 15th to June 15th, both dates inclusive. River Authorities may lengthen the close season as they wish, but they cannot shorten it without byelaw and it must extend over ninety-three days whatever the dates.

Under the terms of the Water Resources Act 1963, the old River Boards of England and Wales are superseded by twenty-eight River Authorities. These, with their addresses, are listed in Appendix II. Each Authority issues its own li-cences to fish, and lays down many rules such as the size of fish that may be retained, hours of fishing, etc. The important thing is the licence. It is sensible to say that you cannot fish anywhere in England or Wales without a River Authority licence. There are odd exceptions but they are best forgotten.

The licence is not all. It is merely a tax on anyone fishing in the area controlled by the Authority. With a very few exceptions it does not entitle you to fish any water anywhere, unless you have another document giving you permission to fish. This document may be a 'ticket' for ticket water owned by an individual, a syndicate or – by far the most common situation – the local angling club.

River Authority licences can usually be obtained from fishing tackle dealers. They will also know what ticket water is available in the area and in many cases will be able to supply tickets.

SCOTLAND

Apart from pike little attention is paid to coarse fish in Scotland. Permission to fish is normally readily granted by riparian owners providing salmon and trout are not unduly disturbed. It is not easy to get local information on coarse fish, but the Scottish Tourist Board publishes annually a booklet on the country's fishing which includes a useful guide to coarse fishing. The Board's address is 2 Rutland Place, West End, Edinburgh 1.

NORTHERN IRELAND

Licences to fish for coarse fish cost 50p a season. They can be obtained from the Fisheries Conservancy Board, 47 Brands Buildings, 49 Donegall Place, Belfast 1.

IRELAND (Republic of)

No licence is required for coarse fishing, nor is there a close season. All that is necessary is the permission of the riparian owner.

ILLEGAL METHODS OF FISHING

The Salmon and Freshwater Fisheries Act has a lengthy Part headed 'Prohibition of certain modes of taking and destroying fish'.

Most of this concerns netting, fish traps, weirs and pollution, but a few items concern the angler.

It is illegal to:

Use *any* fish roe, either as bait or attractor.

Use any light to take fish. This does not apply to the use of a light not directed on the water.

Use any otter, lath or jack (to carry a line out into the river); wire or snare; stroke-haul, snatch or other like instrument (designed to foul-hook fish).

Knowingly take or attempt to take, kill or injure any fish which is unclean or immature. This does not apply to a person who takes a fish accidentally and returns it to the water with the least possible injury.

Disturb any spawn or spawning fish.

J. G. ROBERTS

Tackle

The principal items of coarse fishing tackle are a rod, reel, line and hook, but to these must be added a number of secondary items which include floats, leads, landing net, keep net, rod rests, disgorger and fishing bag or basket.

Many of you will have fished from childhood and know much about rods and tackle. If you are a newcomer to the sport try to take an angler of experience with you when you buy your first major items. If this is not possible, make some inquiries and then go to a recommended and reputable fishing tackle dealer and confide in him. Tell him how much you can afford and ask him if in the slightest doubt about anything. It will be to your advantage if you are not entirely unfamiliar with the sort of thing you should have, so try to remember the following observations about coarse fishing tackle.

RODS

What is now generally known as a bottom fishing rod is the type required, but there are many sorts made for different purposes. Some, unfortunately, are not suitable for any purpose. Rods are made in varying lengths and the popular material is fibre glass, either solid or hollow. Steel rods and built-cane rods are excellent but expensive. Cane (whole) is used for inexpensive rods.

A rod which will be suitable for practically every branch of coarse fishing should be about 11 ft in length and in two pieces, what is now generally known as an 'Avon' rod. The test curve of this type of rod will be in the region of 1 lb but it will not matter if it is a little less than this, the minimum being 12 oz. The test curve is the strain required to bend the rod until the angle formed by the rod and line at the tip, ceases to exist. You can ask your dealer more about this.

'Avon' rods to the original specification are made of built

cane. They are not cheap. Several fibre-glass rods follow the 'Avon' pattern and give excellent service.

Avoid rods made for match fishing if you are going in for general coarse fishing.

REELS

Choose a fixed spool reel, which is the most suitable for practically every branch of coarse fishing. If you are right-handed choose a reel with a left-hand wind, which simply means that

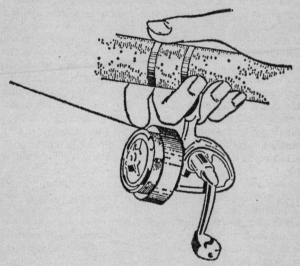

Figure 1 Fixed spool reel. Correct grip

it has its handles on the left-hand side. This enables you to hold the rod in your 'best' hand. If left-handed choose one with a right-hand wind. Fixed spool reels sometimes have two interchangeable spools of different sizes, one to carry a light line and the other a heavy one. If your reel has only one spool it should carry about 100 yds of line which breaks with a 6 lb pull. This will be described as 6 lb breaking strain line. As an accessory to the rod the reel is invaluable when playing a large fish or casting the line any distance. It stores a large quantity of line which can be given or retrieved at will.

LINES

For coarse fishing lines are usually made from either nylon, terylene or other similar synthetic material. A line made from what is known as nylon monofilament is the one most commonly used by coarse fishermen today and is the one you should choose. Unfortunately, many nylon lines are hard and springy and these will give you a lot of trouble if you are fishing with a fixed spool reel, so choose with care.

The strength of your line will depend on many different factors but, as a general rule, fish with one as light as possible, especially if you are on a well-fished water where fish are often extremely shy and avoid a heavy thick line. Do not, however, fish with a line which is so light that many of the fish you hook are going to break it. This applies particularly to weedy or snag-ridden water, as many fish, when hooked, swim at speed to the nearest weed-bed or snag. If your line is too weak you will not be able to stop the fish before it entangles your line in weed stems or roots, pulls on the tight line and breaks it. In weedy water, then, use a line which is heavier than the one you would normally use. This will help to avoid the disappointment of a lost fish. Also you will not be responsible for leaving behind you fish swimming about with hooks in their mouths, not a very pleasant thought and something which should be avoided if at all possible.

The strength of any line or the breaking strain is normally marked on the spool which carries the line and is usually guaranteed by the maker. If the line is subjected to stress above the breaking strain figure it will break. This figure, of course, represents a dead weight breaking strain so any line is capable of landing fish of at least twice the weight of the breaking strain it carries.

The usual method of transferring the line from its spool to the spool of the reel is to tie the line with a double slip-knot to the drum of the reel spool. Get someone to hold the line spool for you and then unwind the line from it by turning the reel handle. Tension must be kept on the line for uniformity of winding and the reel spool should be filled to within about 1/10th of an inch from its edges. If the reel spool is carrying too much line it will cause trouble by unwinding itself and coming off in coils: if too little the line will not readily leave the spool when casting.

HOOKS

These should be chosen with great care although the large assortment in most tackle shops is likely to confuse the beginner. The best plan is to select some of the eyed hooks which are made by most of the well-known tackle manufacturers and you will become more discriminating with experience. Hooks with a round bend or shape are the most suitable, and the thing to look for is a very sharp short point which has the barb close to it. Any coarseness in material should be avoided. Avoid buying hooks which are already whipped or tied to gut as there will then be more potential weak links in your tackle than when using a single knot to tie

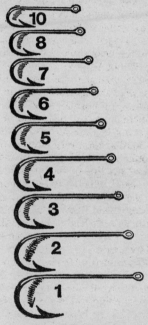

Figure 2 Hooks. Nos 1-10

your reel line direct to the hook. Whippings and loops are often suspect in hooks to gut. They are also much more expensive than eyed hooks.

There is a scale of sizes for coarse fishing hooks which is known as the Redditch scale, hooks being numbered from one to twenty, starting with the small numbers for the largest hooks, as shown in Figure 2. The actual size of hook to use depends on the kind of water you intend to fish, size of fish expected, method of fishing and bait to be used. However, if you always have with you hooks size 8 to 14 you will be equipped to contend with most circumstances.

FLOATS

The majority of coarse fishermen are keen float fishing enthusiasts although, strictly, a float is by no means essential in many branches of the art. Whether of utilitarian value or not, however, most coarse fishermen derive a great deal of satisfaction and pleasure from watching a float cocked on the surface of the water.

The chief functions of a float are to support the baited hook, and any weight which may be attached, above the bed of the lake or river when you are not fishing on the bottom, and also to act as a bite indicator. In other words it should tell you when a fish has taken or is nibbling at your bait.

Floats are often made of quills from geese, swans, crows and porcupines. All of these make excellent floats which can be cut into different sizes to suit various conditions. The bird quills will be suitable for still or quiet waters while a long porcupine or other quill, to which is attached a cork body, will be required in fast water (see Figure 3). Always use a float which is as small and inconspicuous as circumstances will allow. It may only need to be an inch or a little more in length in quiet waters where it will be carrying little or no weight but in a river, when more weight will be required to get the bait down to the fish, it may be 6 ins in length, perhaps even longer.

Avoid floats which have fat and bulbous bodies which offer more resistance to the water than is necessary and choose the slender stream-lined article. Float tops will be painted in different colours to aid visibility at the waterside as there is no one colour which is completely satisfactory for every occasion. Visibility depends to a great extent on background and varies considerably with the different reflections in the water. Red is the best all-round colour but orange and black are also useful, especially during the late evening or against a very dark background. The underpart of a float should be as inconspicuous as possible to help allay the suspicions of fish.

It is usually advisable to attach the float to the line by means of the bottom ring only, especially if the water is weedy. It will then be less likely to become fast in the weeds. Tackle is also more sensitive if this method is adopted. Float

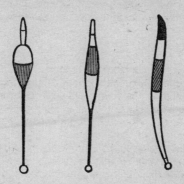

Figure 3 Cork-bodied floats and (right) goose quill float

rings are often whipped directly on to the float but they may be carried separately in a little box, and bicycle valve rubber cut into short lengths is quite suitable for this purpose.

MISCELLANEOUS ITEMS OF TACKLE

A landing net is required to lift a fish from the water after it has been played on rod and line. If a very heavy rod and line were used it would be possible to land a fish without the aid of a net. This is not practical when fishing for the majority of our freshwater fish today as comparatively light tackle must be employed. The dead weight of a fish, of any size, would seriously damage or break this tackle if a net was not available. The landing net is made separate from the handle so the whole can be transported easily. A round net should be at least 15 ins in diameter and the handle not less than 4 ft in length.

The wide assortment of leads used for coarse fishing is illustrated in Figure 4a. There are even more than this. You will, however, need only a few of the many different kinds and this is dealt with more fully later on in this book. Always remember when fishing to use as little lead as circumstances will allow. On many occasions none whatever will be required.

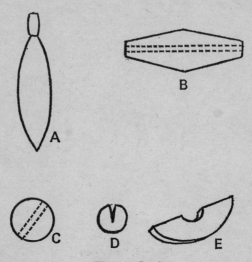

Figure 4a Leads

A. Pear-shaped lead with built-in swivel ('Arlesey Bomb' type). B. Coffin lead. C. Pierced bullet. D. Split shot. E. Foldover or half-moon lead

Keep nets are widely used today for containing and keeping fish alive as they are caught, until they are released at the end of a day's fishing. Keep nets are long nets fitted with metal rings at intervals to keep them open. The bottom is closed and weighted to allow the net to sink in the water, the top is open. There is a line attached to the top of the net which is used for securing it to the bank with a peg and keeping the top above water.

Unfortunately, the practice of keeping live fish imprisoned in a net is a thoroughly bad one and often causes much harm to the fish and the fishery. They often lose scales, sustain bruises and damage themselves if they are in a keep net for any length of time, especially if they are overcrowded. They are usually alive when set free but many only just and these will soon die from disease, which is a result of injury. In my view, a fish, which has already given so much pleasure, should be returned to the water immediately it has been caught.

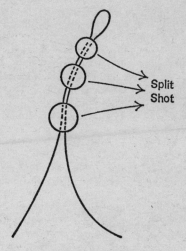

Figure 4b Link ledger

If you feel you *must* keep fish until the end of the day use a very large keep net where overcrowding will be reduced to an absolute minimum. This applies particularly to bream which seem to be weak fish that succumb very quickly when kept in captivity.

Sometimes a hook may become so embedded in a fish's mouth or gullet that it will be impossible to extract it with the fingers. When this happens a disgorger may be used for taking out the hook. A disgorger is usually made from a long piece of wire with a vee-shaped slot or spiral at one end. The line passes through the slot which is then pushed down on to the hook to free it. Surgical forceps are excellent for this purpose but are rather expensive. Normally it is possible to extract a hook from a fish without the aid of a disgorger but this must be done with great care, causing as little damage as possible to the fish. The fish must be held firmly, but not roughly, by placing the left hand over its back in about the centre. The hook can then be removed with the finger and thumb of the right hand. Prevent at all costs fish jumping about on the bank as this causes bruising and scale removal, which are the forerunners of disease.

It is not necessary in many branches of coarse fishing to hold the rod in the hand when fishing, so the rod is usually placed in a rod rest or rests which are stuck into the ground in a convenient position.

Small items of fishing tackle can be carried in little boxes and the whole in a fishing bag or basket. Wicker baskets for coarse fishing are roomy and may be used as seats but they are clumsy and often cause much inconvenience when travelling, particularly on public transport. A fishing bag or haversack is a more practical proposition than a basket and the seat can be a separate folding stool which is easy to carry. The bag should be roomy and made from proofed canvas, twill or some other waterproof material.

(On p 68 Capt. L. A. Parker strongly advocates a basket instead of a bag. He is writing only about roach fishing, where the angler has normally to be seated for long periods as motionless as possible. The tackle basket is designed as a seat, which is ideal for this purpose. Mr Roberts writes about coarse fishing generally, and in much of that fishing the angler may be frequently on the move, so he prefers a bag to the rather awkward basket. [Ed.])

TACKLE MAKING

It is quite possible to make first-class fishing tackle at home and this includes rods as well as most other items of an angler's equipment. Tackle making is an absorbing pastime, particularly suitable for long winter evenings, and the result can mean a considerable saving in money when compared with the shop-bought manufactured article. Exceptional skill or a great number of tools are not required.

I suggest that anyone interested in this matter study *Fly Tying, Rod and Tackle Making*, published by Barrie & Jenkins.

CARE OF TACKLE

A good rod will, with proper care, last a lifetime and a reel for a great number of years. Guard against damp, so always take the rod out of its bag after use and rub down when dry. It can again be rubbed over with a rag soaked in linseed oil. A rod should not be left leaning against a wall but placed horizontally across supporting pegs. If this is not possible the joints should be hung vertically from a nail. It needs only a rubber ring to hold them together and to suspend them. Examine the varnish, rings and ferrules from time to time and repaint when necessary without delay. The ferrules or joints should be kept absolutely clean and lubricated. Corks are often pushed into the female ferrule to keep out grit and dirt. The main essentials with rod joints are cleanliness and lubrication, if these are neglected they will stick and cause much trouble.

A container made of aluminium or a similar light alloy is useful for protecting a rod when travelling, especially when going on holiday or making a long journey. A rod, however, should never be stored in a case because air should be allowed to circulate around it.

The reel should be oiled occasionally with thin oil according to the maker's instructions and kept scrupulously clean as grit and dirt are abrasive and can seriously damage the mechanism. Never rest your reel on the bare ground when fishing but put a waterproof sheet under it and protect it as much as possible against rain and other sources of damp. Smaller but no less important items of fishing tackle should be examined most carefully after each fishing trip and repaired or renewed when necessary.

Lines and hooks require particular attention and should be rejected if suspect and replaced as soon as possible. The end of a fishing line sometimes becomes frayed and weak but even if there are no visible signs of stress it is wise to cut off and discard a yard or two from the end from time to time. Hooks cannot be too sharp and may be pointed with a file or carborundum stone when necessary; learn to become hook-minded as, strangely enough, this is one item of tackle which many anglers neglect. Try to acquire the habit of inspecting the hook frequently when actually fishing. Attention to these small details will help you to fish more efficiently and avoid disappointments in the form of lost fish.

ASSEMBLY

This will be done at the waterside when the natural urge will be to hurry and commence fishing as soon as possible. Guard against this however and assemble your tackle with care and without hurry. Make sure the joints are properly fitted, the rings are in line and the reel secure, thread the line carefully through each ring and do not commence fishing if you discover that you have accidentally missed one; take off the float and hook and rethread the line through all the rings. The half blood knot should be used to tie the hook to line. The line-to-hook connexion is all that is needed and the rest of the line should be without knot or join. If you do discover a fault in

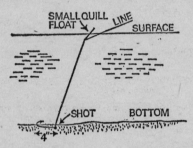

Figure 5 Arrangement of terminal tackle when fishing in calm water

your line cut well above it and discard. Never tie pieces of broken line together except in emergency. Line joints are a potential source of weakness and the only join necessary is that which connects line with hook. Simplicity should be the keynote with all fishing tackle.

When the rod is assembled never leave it lying on the ground where someone could easily tread on it, but lean it against a bush or tree. When walking with a rod always have the butt in front, this will prevent the fragile tip from accidentally hitting the ground and getting damaged. A rubber band may be used for securing the hook when moving from one place to another and this can be placed around the rod butt.

Finally, do not despair if you are unable to afford the best tackle and do not be put off by all the paraphernalia and expensive-looking equipment you will almost certainly see at the waterside. Much of this is quite unnecessary anyway. Buy the best you can afford and learn as much as you can about the ways and habits of the fish you seek. This is much more important than possessing an expensive rod and reel.

The following figures show various arrangements of tackle for different conditions and methods.

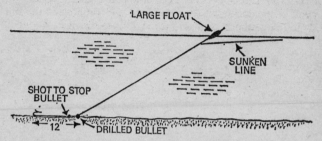

Figure 6 Float ledgering tackle for roach suitable in rough weather. Note hook now 12 ins. from lead

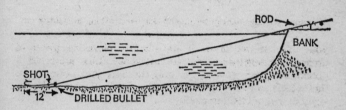

Figure 7 Ledgering without a float

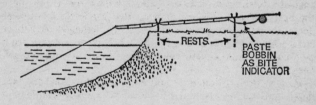

Figure 8 Rod in rests with piece of bread paste as bite indicator

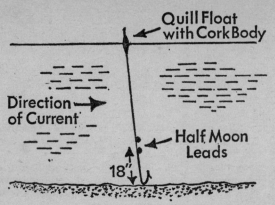

Figure 9 Swimming the stream with bait just off the bottom. Shot, bunched together at least 18 ins. from hook, may be used instead of half-moon leads

FRANK OATES

Baits and Groundbaits

So many different baits have led to the capture of coarse fish that is is impossible to deal at length with all of them, nor do the several freak baits merit attention.

In this section the three main baits – maggots, worms and bread (including pastes) – are discussed comprehensively. Hemp seed, wasp grubs, wheat and live baits are each dealt with, briefly, and the remainder are grouped.

Groundbaits are as important as hook baits in coarse fishing, and their composition and preparation is described in detail.

MAGGOTS

Four species of maggots are in general use today. These are 'livers', larvae of the bluebottle; 'pinkies', larvae of the greenbottle; 'squats', larvae of the common house-fly; and 'specials', larvae of a less common fly. Most popular of the above four species are 'livers' which can be bought at almost every fishing tackle dealer's shop in the country, or by post from any of the well-known breeders who advertise in the angling press.

'Pinkies' and 'squats' can also be obtained by post. 'Specials' can rarely be purchased, and for a regular supply of these you must breed them yourself.

Your choice of maggots will depend on the type of waters you intend to fish and also the species of fish you are after. The quantity you will need to feed your swim will be ruled by the area and depth of water and the size of the fish in it.

Generally speaking, for large deep waters containing big fish you will need large quantities of 'livers', but in small, shallow waters populated by very small fish, only a few of the smaller maggots such as 'pinkies' or 'squats' will be needed.

These two latter species are often used, however, in conjunction with ground bait to feed large deep swims when after big fish. 'Pinkies' and 'squats' are then used in large quantities.

The more careful you are in the preparation of your maggots before use the better your results will be. Buy them from the dealer's about a week before you need to use them so that you have every opportunity of getting them into perfect condition for your proposed outing.

Cleaning Maggots

Every bit of sawdust should at once be riddled out so that nothing but maggots remains. Then half fill an old bowl or box with damp sand, and scatter the maggots evenly over the surface. If this is done under a strong light or out in the sunlight the maggots will soon disappear from view, leaving large pieces of sawdust, skins and chrysalises on the surface. Scrape these off with a table knife and throw out.

After a few days scouring in the sand the bodies of the maggots will be thoroughly cleaned and free from grease, ensuring that they sink straight to the bottom of the deepest swim. Any food still in them when they arrive from the breeders (which usually shows as a dark patch underneath the skin) will also disappear during scouring in the sand, giving them a clean, mellow appearance. All traces of ammonia gases will also have been removed. This is essential, for these gases sicken the fish, putting them off feed.

Keep in a cool place, and all you have to do before fishing is to empty sand and maggots on to a riddle for separating. Shake the sand through and you will be left with maggots only.

Wash thoroughly under a cold-water tap. Put about half a pint of maggots at a time in a bowl-shaped culinary sieve and after a good swilling to get every vestige of remaining dust and dirt out of them, tap out surplus water and empty them on to one half of an old towel. By placing the other half on top and gently rolling them with the palms of your hands you can dry them off and tip them into a clean tin ready for use (Figure 10). Pick out the largest for use on the hook. These can be coloured with chrysiodine powder to an attractive shade of primrose yellow.

The 'liver' maggots are now in perfect condition for use, clean and polished and looking really appetizing to fish. Those left for feeding the swim can be thrown in loose, or squeezed inside lumps of ground bait, but either way they will quickly sink to the bed of the swim.

To make a good catch of fish you must always have a liberal

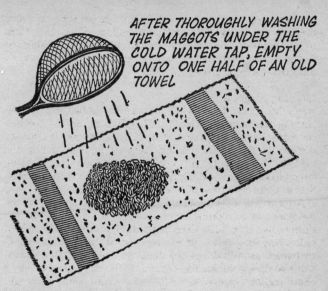

AFTER THOROUGHLY WASHING THE MAGGOTS UNDER THE COLD WATER TAP, EMPTY ONTO ONE HALF OF AN OLD TOWEL

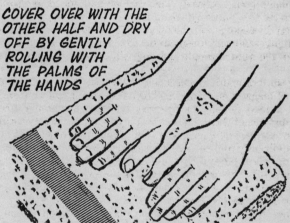

COVER OVER WITH THE OTHER HALF AND DRY OFF BY GENTLY ROLLING WITH THE PALMS OF THE HANDS

Figure 10

supply of maggots to feed your swim on the 'little and often' principle, for it is a fact that, within reason, the more maggots you throw into your swim, the more fish you can expect to take out. The amount of maggots you take to the waterside, however, is often governed by how many you can afford and not by how many you think you will need, for maggots are an expensive item, which is the reason why so many anglers breed their own. When after such fish as barbel, bream and chub you need half a gallon of maggots at least to ensure a good catch.

Breeding Maggots
All maggots are easily bred during the summer months if you have access to an outbuilding on an allotment or piece of land at a reasonable distance away from habitation.

'Livers' and 'Pinkies'
For 'livers' or 'pinkies', you need a few shallow trays in which to place the meat, usually bought from the knackers', such as sheep's heads, cat and dog meat, etc, but fowls and rabbits will also do. The best maggots, however, are bred on liver.

The shed windows should be well shaded with sacking to darken the inside. A suitable piece of meat hung up outside in a tree on a warm sunny day will soon collect plenty of 'blows', or eggs, which you then transfer on to the remaining meat, The point to be careful about is not to put too many eggs on each piece of meat in the trays. A patch the size of a penny is ample for each 7 lb of meat. Sawdust is laid round the edges of the trays for the maggots to bury into when they leave the meat (Figure 11). Place sacking over the top to prevent any more 'blows' from appearing, for you do not want the meat to be all eaten before the maggots are fully grown.

'Pinkies' can be bred in exactly the same way as 'livers', and you often get both species breeding together on the same piece of meat, but they prefer fish. If you put the fish heads and trimmings down in your trays you will be able to produce plenty of good quality 'pinkies'.

'Specials'
'Specials' are bred by putting scalded bran into breeding trays and pouring sour milk over the surface of the bran with a few small bits of fish pushed underneath.

Place these trays on shelves in the darkest part of the shed.

BREEDING TRAY
WITH PIECE OF MEAT
SURROUNDED BY SAWDUST
FOR MAGGOTS TO RETIRE TO
WHEN FULLY FED

SAWDUST
SHOULD
BE RIDDLED
VERY FINE
BEFORE USE
IN BREEDING
TRAYS

Figure 11

The 'blows' will soon appear and in ten days the resulting pure white maggots will be fully matured.

If you can manage to put down a tray once a week throughout the summer months (using the first ones, of course, again as soon as you empty them) you will have a regular supply of 'specials' to keep you going all through the season.

'Squats'

'Squats' are usually gathered from large refuse heaps and from matter cleared from piggeries and stables. 'Squats' can be bred artificially provided you maintain the temperature around 21°C (70°F) and provide them with quantities of stable and piggery refuse, and keep them in the dark under cover.

Other types of refuse such as the droppings from poultry houses will usually be full of 'squats' throughout the summer months.

You can therefore try different mediums in your trays, and you will find that certain mixings will attract and breed only certain types of flies. These experiments are interesting and full of possibilities.

Other Maggots

Rotting vegetable matter mixed up with bone meal and placed in trays to a depth of 2 ins or so will attract another species of fly whose larvae make very deadly hook baits. If you study the various types of flies in their natural breeding grounds and set about producing them artificially, it is surprising what a fine supply of bait you can produce. You do need a really liberal supply of such deadly baits as 'pinkies' and 'squats' to feed your swim lavishly on the 'little and often' principle, for this is the real secret behind those huge catches of coarse fish you read about in the angling press.

Chrysalises

When dealing with fairly large quantities of maggots one cannot prevent a certain number turning into chrysalises. Do not throw these away for they are another very deadly bait in themselves, and in very hot weather, especially during midday, chrysalises are often the only bait that will tempt the fish to feed. Use them in your groundbait just the same as maggots for feeding the swim and use one chrysalis on your smallest hook, say a size 20 or 18. Most species of fish will take chrysalises, especially roach and bleak.

Hooking a Maggot

It is essential that your maggot remains very lively on the hook, and consequently you should be very careful about the way you impale it. If you look at the broad end of a maggot very closely you will see two 'eyes', and above these a small protuberance containing the vent, and it is in the vent that your hook point should be inserted and brought lightly out

Figure 12 Enlarged view of maggot, showing vent at the top where hook point should be inserted

again leaving the point quite uncovered and ready for action.

If you sharpen your hooks you will find that impaling the maggot is very simple indeed, and you will rarely ever burst it with the hook point or barb; but if you do happen to burst open the skin and spill out the white inside, take another and start again.

The accompanying illustration shows where you can find the vent (Figure 12).

Cooked Maggots

Cooked maggots proved very successful as a groundbait for bream during the years when bread groundbait was banned from use, and today quite a number of successful bream anglers still pin their faith to cooked maggots.

They are prepared by first half-filling a bucket with water and then heating it. When the water is boiling a couple of pints of best quality liver maggots are quickly dropped in and stirred briskly to ensure they are all instantly killed.

Their insides will at once be cooked like the white of an egg. The maggots are stretched out quite straight and are half as long again as their original length. Their cooked insides show

Figure 13 Cooked maggots. Make sure water is really boiling, then drop in and stir very quickly

through their skins giving them an attractive snowy-white appearance. While cooking a very appetizing, creamy, nutty aroma arises, the scent of which from cooked maggots proves extremely attractive to bream.

After cooking the bulk of the maggots will sink to the bottom of the bucket, which should be lifted off the heat as soon as all the maggots are cooked, a process which takes only two or three minutes after dropping them in. A small percentage will be found floating on the top and these are usually the smaller ones and those which have been fed on poor quality meat. These floaters should be skimmed off and thrown away, for at the waterside they will only float to the surface and spoil your swim.

The sunken maggots are now poured into a clean muslin bag or pillow case and hung up to let the bulk of the water drain out. They are taken down in a few minutes, while still quite wet, and stored in a very cool place until ready for use, when they are fed into the swim with the aid of ground bait in the usual way. They quickly spread out on the river bed to make a white carpet, and it will not be long before the bream find them and, scavengers as they are, they soon make short work of these cooked dead maggots. Use two or three cooked maggots on your hook.

Liver-bred Maggots
Maggots bred on liver are generally acknowledged as the best you can buy, for there is something about the taste of liver-bred maggots that is irresistible to the palates of most coarse fish.

Liver-bred maggots are easily recognizable by their natural butter-yellow colour, which is in itself a great attraction to fish. Consequently, when you buy your maggots or receive them by mail, spend a little time selecting a couple of hundred or so of the plump yellow-hued ones for use as hook baits. The rest are of course used in your groundbait.

Storing and Carrying
Maggots should always be stored in as cool a place as possible and the best place of all is in a refrigerator. Failing this, many anglers bury them in the garden inside a strong tin with very tiny air holes, where they will keep in good condition for several days or even weeks.

When maggots have to be transported long distances during very hot weather they quickly turn into chrysalises. Consequently they should be suffocated while still cool before setting off. Fruit bottling jars are ideal for this purpose but any airtight container will do. The maggots are packed into the jars which are filled right to the top. The lids are then screwed down tightly. In an hour or so the maggots will stop wriggling and lie prostrate. They can then be safely carried over long distances during the hottest weather, for there is no activity from their bodies and they will remain cool in the angler's basket.

They can be thus imprisoned up to twenty-four hours with perfect safety and although they may look dead, they are far from it. On arriving at the waterside, unscrew the bottle tops and empty out the suffocated maggots into a pillow case or similar clean cloth bag. Then spread it out flat on the grass to catch the wind and the sun, when the maggots will revive in about ten to twenty minutes (according to the temperature) and be in perfect condition again for fishing.

Numbers Required

The question of how many maggots are required for successfully feeding any particular swim cannot be answered by hard-and-fast rules, as the amounts vary with each type of water and with the species of fish inhabiting the swim.

The size of the feeder maggots, ie, 'squats', 'pinkies' or gentles, has also to be adjusted to suit different waters and the species of fish likely to be encountered. In summer, with water temperatures around 10°C (55°F) and over, most fish feed very freely. Then, in well-stocked waters, generous feeding can give excellent results.

In winter, however, just the opposite is the case, for in water temperatures below 5°C (40°F) and down to nearly freezing-point, the few fish which do not hibernate lie in a semi-torpid state in the deepest water and hardly feed at all. Consequently, in these conditions, one good handful of maggots thrown in can ruin your chances of catching anything at all. So you must use your judgement and feed heavily when conditions and size of waters and fish require it and not at all when they do not.

'Pinkies' are well suited for the smaller fry which inhabit lakes and wide sluggish rivers, because being fairly heavy they can be thrown much farther than squats. When after small fry loose maggots seem to be more deadly than when used in groundbait, for with the latter you cannot help making a slight disturbance on the surface but loose feeders fall silently like rain and are very deadly.

Feeding with 'pinkies' during the summer months at the rate of one pint per hour soon collects large numbers of small fry, which at times make the water surface 'boil' in their eagerness to get there first. One solid pint of 'pinkies' without sawdust will contain approximately 8,000, and they will go a long way when feeding the swim on the 'little and often' principle, which is a really sure way of collecting a good shoal of fish. A small handful thrown in, say, once every minute without exception is just about right.

In the rivers with water speeds of one to two miles per hour liver maggots come into their own, for they are large and heavy and will quickly sink into the larger and deeper swims.

TYPES TO AVOID

Small white-looking maggots should always be avoided if possible, for they are bred on offal and bones, usually of very poor quality. A large percentage of them float, which makes them practically useless to the angler. It is advisable, therefore, to make a point of finding out where you can buy the best quality and then stick to that source; for good-quality maggots make all the difference to your results at the waterside.

Maggots are the number one bait with the majority of match anglers, and at each National Angling Championship the thousand or more competitors throw in well over 500 gallons of feeder maggots, which works out on an average at about four pints per competitor for five hours' fishing. When you are fishing a wide river which is known to contain plenty of large fish, do not be afraid to feed on a lavish scale with feeders and groundbait.

WORMS

The next baits in order of importance available to the coarse fish angler are worms. The three most useful and most popular are lobworms, red worms (ie brandlings, marsh worms, gilt tails, etc) and bloodworms. The last named are not related in any way to the earthworms, for they are the larvae of the common gnat or midge, but for convenience they are dealt with in this chapter.

Lobworms

Lobworms have accounted for many big fish, including several record holders in the British list at one time or another, and are definitely a first-class bait for use by the specimen hunter. Lobworms have also accounted for many huge catches of barbel in years gone by when it was common practice to bait up the swim with thousands of lobs and to keep this up for several successive days prior to the day of fishing, when catches often proved enormous.

The recognized way of baiting up the hook was to thread

35

the lob on to the gut with a baiting needle, pulling it down the gut to the hook, a method which still cannot be improved upon (Figure 14).

Collecting Lobworms

Lobworms can be collected after dark on warm damp evenings with the aid of a torch or lamp, when they can be seen on close-cut lawns, footpaths and garden borders, laid out on the surface with their tails inside their burrows. The art of collecting them is to move about noiselessly, for they will disappear at the slightest sound. The beam from the light does not affect them, and all you have to do is to grip them as close to the hole as possible and pull them gently but firmly out of the burrow. It requires a little practice, for if you do not get a proper grip on them they will retreat through your fingers like a flash, and once they are more than halfway down again it is impossible to extract them without breaking them.

Another method is to trap them by the head and hold them down tightly to the ground, when their resulting struggles usually swing their bodies right out of the burrow.

Storing Lobworms

Lobworms can be stored at the bottom of the garden in an old tub or wooden box let into the soil flush with the surface and covered with sacking. Any lobs you do not use after fishing can be brought back to the tub to save for another day. The tub should be filled with light, black loamy soil together with a few leaves and moss. It is a simple matter to lift out a couple of forkfuls when you need a few lobworms.

Another method of storing worms is to fill a bucket with sphagnum moss, which can be bought at a florists quite cheaply. The lobworms are simply tipped on to the moss and they then work their way through, cleaning and toughening themselves as they go. The surface of the moss should now be well sprinkled with water until thoroughly damp, when the moisture will gradually soak through to the bottom. Keep the moss damp by sprinkling lightly with water each evening. Every two or three days the bucket should be emptied out and the worms sorted. Remove the dead ones, for if these are allowed to remain they will quickly destroy the others. If you do this regularly you can keep your worms in perfect condition for a long time. The bucket should be securely covered at night.

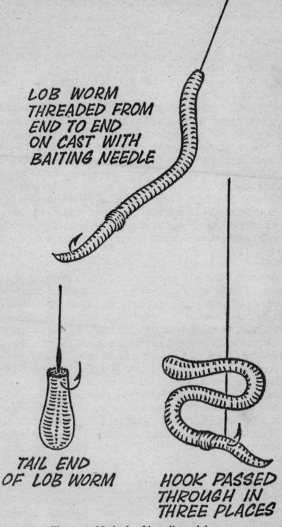

LOB WORM
THREADED FROM
END TO END
ON CAST WITH
BAITING NEEDLE

TAIL END
OF LOB WORM

HOOK PASSED
THROUGH IN
THREE PLACES

Figure 14 Methods of impaling a lobworm

Red Worms
Red worms are another very popular and deadly bait for
coarse fish, and especially so during the winter months. The
term red worms embraces several species, the three most
common being brandlings, marsh worms and gilt tails. These,
too, can be purchased from leading fishing tackle dealers or by
post from advertisers in the angling press.

Collecting Brandlings
Brandlings are generally found just under the surface around
the edges of large refuse heaps and it is a simple matter to turn
over the surface with a fork and collect an ample supply for a
day's sport. They can be found at times so thickly that one
forkful of soil turned over will uncover hundreds of brandlings all clinging together, sufficient to fill your tin in a matter
of five minutes.

Brandlings can be bred at home if you arrange a small
wormery at the bottom of your garden by sinking a tub into
the soil and filling it with a mixture of loam and refuse including rotting vegetable matter such as cabbage stalks, leaves,
etc. Put a supply of brandlings in the tub, cover the surface
with sacking and keep moist by watering gently in the evenings when needed. The worms will breed quickly and you will
always have a regular supply.

Brandlings and marsh worms lay approximately 400 eggs a
year. They are laid in small batches close to the surface and
within 2 ins of food. The parents remain with the eggs until
they hatch a week after laying. One month later the young
worms are large enough to serve as bait on small hooks.

As Hook and Groundbait
Brandlings are good for many types of coarse fish and can be
used in your groundbait just the same as maggots. They are
easily and quickly impaled on the hook by inserting the point
at two or three places and drawing the nylon through.
Another way is to attach the worm to the hook by the head
end only, a method used by match anglers when after perch,
etc. It is a very deadly method providing you are not too
quick on the strike (Figure 15).

Brandlings on an average are 2 to 3 ins long and only about
one-third the size of lobworms. They are usually used in
fishing for medium-sized roach, dace, perch and bream.

Many match anglers today use maggot bait exclusively

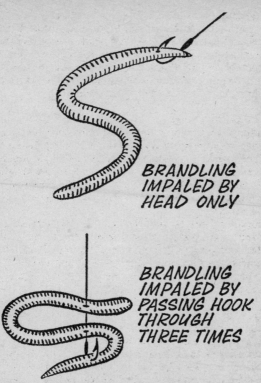

BRANDLING
IMPALED BY
HEAD ONLY

BRANDLING
IMPALED BY
PASSING HOOK
THROUGH
THREE TIMES

Figure 15 Two methods of attaching brandling worms

wherever they go. They have become so used to this practice that they rarely think of taking any worms or paste to use as an alternative bait in case the fish are difficult to lure with maggots. This is a bad practice, for there are numerous places containing certain species which are seldom tempted by maggots. Even on the venues where maggots usually prove best, there are times, especially towards the end of a contest when fish become exceptionally difficult to tempt, and when a change of bait is likely to give results.

At the large open events it is surprising to learn how many well-known experts are content to carry maggots only, especially on waters that contain shoals of good perch, a fish that nearly always prefers a red worm.

In team contests anglers should carry at least three different hook baits if they are determined to pull their weight and make sure they scrape up every possible ounce from their allotted swim.

Change of Bait

Often towards the end of a contest fish become extremely difficult to lure: then is the time to change over to red worms and try to get those extra few ounces which make all the difference to the final team result. A change to red worms gave surprising results to Mr F. Love when fishing a 70-strong Northampton Nene club match on the Great Ouse at Newton Blossomville. His swim was the last one downstream and, starting as usual with maggots, he fished for a long time with very poor results, so he changed over to red worms and quickly ran into a large bream. At the end of the contest he had piled into three keep nets a catch of 49 lb 13 oz, his best bream weighing 5 lb 12 oz. Only one roach was included in this fine catch, but it weighed 1 lb 3 oz, proving that good roach can be tempted by a red worm. All these fish were caught on size 14 hooks.

When a change over to worms is made, a larger-sized hook to the usual 18 and 20 size maggot hooks is necessary, and it is well worth the time taken to slip off the maggot hook and put back a larger size for worm fishing.

When using worms, the strike must never be too hurried and a taking fish must be given more time than is usual with maggots. Careful casting is also necessary, for worms will not 'stay put' as long as maggots unless they are threaded on with a baiting needle.

Bloodworms

Bloodworms, larvae of the common gnat, are a killing and deadly bait indeed for most species of coarse fish, especially roach. They are little over $\frac{1}{2}$ inch in length and can often be seen on the surface of rainwater butts, looping and straightening as they swim to and fro. Their best breeding grounds, however, are in the black mud found around larger sewage works, and in the banks of tidal waterways, streams, ditches and swamps. They are collected by scooping up the mud in a fine-mesh net and then pouring water into the net, swilling the mud through until only the bloodworms remain. These are then dropped into a can of water and the process repeated until sufficient have been collected.

Red moulders' sand, suitably damped, is often used as a medium for sinking bloodworms to the bottom of a swim for ground bait, but they can, of course, be mixed with other ground bait in the usual way.

Use on Hook

The largest bloodworms are picked out for the hook, which should be no bigger than a size 20 and well sharpened, for bloodworms are very fragile and easily burst. The correct way to impale bloodworms on the hook is to lay the worm out flat on your finger and insert the hook point through the head end very carefully (Figure 16). A little practice is needed to master this delicate operation.

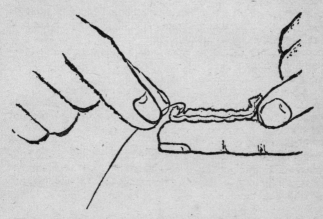

Figure 16 Method of impaling bloodworm. Insert hook point in head segment, turning hook through very gently after feeling point come through on forefinger

There are special hooks available for use with bloodworms, made in a very fine flat wire, in very small sizes. Your dealer can order them if he does not stock them.

Storing

Bloodworms can be stored in a cool place in glass jars containing a little water. The water has to be changed fairly frequently to keep them in perfect condition.

BREAD AND PASTES

Bread is a popular and widely used bait which has accounted for several record fish, including the record carp of 44 lb, caught on a mixture of paste and bread crust.

Plain Paste

The simplest way to make bread paste is to cut a fairly thick slice from a white loaf. Remove the crusts and break up into about six pieces. Place in the centre of a clean white cloth and cover with a sprinkling of sugar. The corners of the cloth are now gathered up and the centre portion containing the bread is twisted into a ball and dipped quickly into boiling water. Then knead the bread vigorously with the fingers until it is as pliable as putty, when it is ready for moulding on the hook.

When used on, say, a number 14 hook for roach and bream in a well groundbaited swim, bread paste can account for huge catches of fish. The bites, however, are a little on the slow side. The float often trembles for several minutes before the fish takes the paste right inside its mouth and it is for this reason that paste is rarely used for competition fishing, but for all other fishing it is definitely first-class and accounts for some really big fish.

Flake

Bread flake is a piece of white bread pulled from the centre of the loaf and squeezed round the hook. Although it requires a little more skill in handling the tackle to prevent it from coming off the hook, it is a much quicker and more deadly bait then bread paste.

Bread Cubes

Bread cubes are also an excellent bait and just as effective as flake. The cubes are cut from the base of the loaf where the bread is a little firmer and stronger. The size of the cubes varies according to taste, say from $\frac{1}{2}$ inch to 1 inch. They are impaled on the hook in the usual way and are generally used for swimming down the stream for roach and dace.

Cheese Paste

Cheese paste is made similarly to bread paste as described above, but before gathering up the cloth rub a piece of cheese

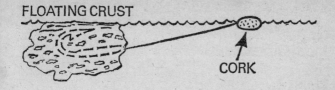

FLOATING CRUST

CORK

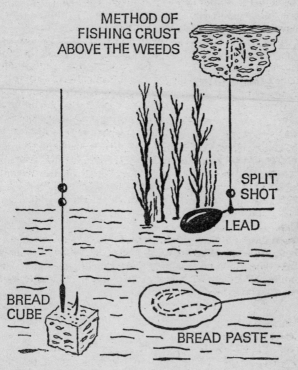

METHOD OF
FISHING CRUST
ABOVE THE WEEDS

SPLIT
SHOT

LEAD

BREAD
CUBE

BREAD PASTE

Figure 17 Some methods of baiting with bread crust and bread paste

on a grater over the bread until there is a liberal covering of
cheese parings.

Alternatively, cheese paste can be made from the pure
cheese alone, by cutting a piece from the main cheese and
kneading this up until it is soft and pliable and easily

moulded on to the hook. You can also use processed cheeses wrapped in lead foil, which can be carried in the fishing box in their wrappers ready for use at any time they are needed.

Cheese paste is a recognized bait for large chub and barbel, and when a walnut-sized piece is fished right down on the river bed where these fish are known to be, there is no knowing what size of fish you are likely to hit.

The three most important points to watch when using paste baits are consistency, size and shape. Anglers differ greatly as to the right consistency. The majority agree that these pastes should be stiff enough to remain on the hook, but not so stiff as to prejudice hook penetration.

Soft Pastes

Some successful match anglers swear by extremely soft pastes, necessitating frequent rebaiting of the hook. These tactics, however, are mostly confined to canals where underhand casting is all that is needed.

Many successful paste anglers stick a small lump of paste on the butt of the rod, just above the handle, so that a finger may be drawn through it and the hook baited by wiping it against the paste-smeared fingers. Some anglers who use this extra soft paste like to work a little cotton wool into it, sufficient to make it remain on the hook while casting.

Sizes of paste baits vary from a 'pin head' up to pieces as large as a walnut, acording to the type of water and species of fish, the biggest pieces usually being for 'laying on' or ledgering, and the smaller pieces for midwater fishing.

Flavoured and Coloured Pastes

As mentioned above, chub and barbel like a good big lump and both show a definite liking for paste flavoured with cheese.

Carp and tench show a preference for paste flavoured with honey and also sometimes for paste made with brown bread.

Pastes can be coloured to any required shade by dye powders. Many anglers sprinkle custard powder on bread before mixing or kneading to give it added flavour and a yellow tint.

There are several flavourings, too, which can be mixed into paste, such as oil of aniseed and oil of rhodium. Lists of these dyes and flavourings are given in the section so headed.

HEMP SEED

Hemp seed is perhaps the most deadly and the best bite-producing bait known to the coarse fishing world, and it is only the fact that it is banned on many waters that prevents it from rivalling the maggot as the 'number one coarse fish bait'.

Hemp seed, being an oily food, is fairly filling; consequently, although you must feed the swim on the 'little and often' principle to collect a large shoal of fish, never throw in large handfuls or you will put the fish off feed. About twenty seeds once every minute is about right. Pitch them to the head of the swim in running water and you will soon have the surface boiling with fish.

You can buy hemp seed from the majority of fishing tackle dealers and by post from firms advertising in the angling press.

Preparation

To prepare hemp seed for fishing, soak it in a bowl of cold water overnight, then place in a saucepan and just cover with water. Place the pan on heat, bring it to the boil and then let it gently simmer for about ten minutes until the grains split and show a thin line of white inside.

Remove a couple of tablespoonfuls of these for the hook and then continue to simmer the remainder for another twenty minutes until they are showing a lot more of the white inside. These will now serve admirably for groundbaiting the swim.

Hooking Hemp Seed

Hooks made from flat wire are the best for baiting with hemp seed. Push the back or the bend of the hook into the white split where the seed has burst. If you squeeze the hemp seed as tightly as possible before pushing in the hook the seed will grip on to the bend of the hook on releasing the pressure.

Never insert the point of the hook into the white split for you will surely hit the hard seed case and most likely blunt the point of your hook. Even if you did bring the point right through the seed, it is so hard that, lying on the inside of the shank, it would tend to stop the hook point penetrating and being driven right home on the strike. If the bend is pushed into the white split as described above, the hook will leave the seed instantly as you strike.

Hemp seed is a clean and perfect bait which can provide really exciting sport, not only with roach and dace but with bream and barbel. Many a fine barbel has fallen to hemp.

Striking with Hemp Seed

When using hemp one has to be very quick on the strike, for the bites are as quick as lightning. Consequently it is a very sound idea to get into the habit of drawing your tackle slowly through the water with your rod point immediately after casting so that then your line will always be straight from hook to float, and when the bite occurs you will be in direct contact with your hook and will rarely miss.

Lead Wire

Another point to watch is to use lead wire on your cast instead of shots, for the latter are often mistaken by the fish for hemp seeds, resulting in a lot of false bites, which of course you miss, until you begin to wonder if your reflexes are letting you down. By weighting the cast with a short length of lead wire spiraled round tightly to prevent it slipping, false bites will be avoided (Figure 18).

History

Hemp seed was first introduced into this country during the 1914–18 war by some Belgian refugees. The bait caught on quickly. Later, after it had swept the country, it was the cause of much controversy and many anglers claimed that it was a drug and harmful to the fish. Many clubs passed rules prohibiting its use on club waters. It was proved later by authorities at the British Natural History Museum and elsewhere that hemp seed was a perfectly wholesome food and had no harmful effects on fish. Even so, hemp seed still remains banned on several waters.

Very large catches of roach have been made with hemp seed. The discredited theory of its deadliness was that it contained a narcotic drug. It is now generally assumed that fish mistake hemp seeds for small freshwater molluscs.

However, the fact remains that it is a really excellent bait, clean to handle and easy to prepare. If you want good sport and big catches of fish you cannot have a better bait than hemp seed.

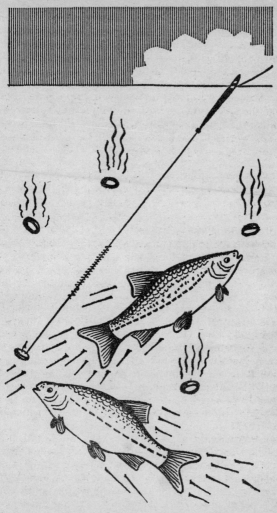

Figure 18 To prevent false bites when hemp seed fishing, use lead wire on the cast and not split shots. Also, keep the float moving to ensure the line is always tight

WASP GRUBS

Wasp grubs are an excellent bait for most coarse fish, especially chub and dace. They are larger than the liver maggot, but they are also much softer and consequently have to be handled and attached to the hook more carefully.

Like all the above-mentioned baits you need them in sufficient quantity to feed the swim on the 'little and often' principle, say a dozen or so once every minute all the time you are fishing. They can be thrown in loose or used in conjunction with ground bait.

There are a fair number of fishing tackle shops where wasp grubs can be purchased, and also plenty of countrymen such as gardeners and gamekeepers who dig out wasps' nest in the season and with whom a keen angler can come to some arrangement.

Collecting Wasp Grubs

You can also take a nest yourself without any fear of getting stung if you set about the job in a proper manner. Liquid cyanide has been the recognized medium for taking wasp nests for several years, but it is dangerous stuff. Today there are several new chemicals available for killing wasps, both in liquid or powder form. They can be bought from chemists and are much safer products to handle than cyanide. They quickly kill everything inside the nest and leave the grubs in perfect condition for fishing.

Having bought your wasp destroyer you must find a nest, and this is done by careful observation on a summer's evening starting, say, a couple of hours before sunset, for that is the time when wasps are homeward bound. Take note of the direction in which the majority are flying, and gradually follow them up until you finally track down their nest.

Banks, hedgerows and the banks of streams and ponds are all likely places to find wasps' nests, and once you have had a little practice in tracking them down you will be surprised to learn how easy it is to find them and how many nests there are.

The best time to attack a wasps' nest is after sunset, when they have retired for the night. For quite a time after the sun has set there will still be sufficient light for you to see what you are doing. Follow the instructions on the package or bottle. In some cases the hole must be left open: in others it must be blocked.

Preparation

Next morning you can dig out the nest with perfect safety and place all the cakes and any bits that might fall off into a basket. On arriving home, spread the cakes out on newspapers and separate all the grubs from the cakes and place them in a clean tin, throwing away the broken cakes and mature wasps.

Hook Baits and Groundbait

Pick out a hundred or so of the best grubs for the hook. These are the fat, juicy, yellowish ones that show no signs of either legs or wings. Some anglers try to toughen these hook baits by baking them in the oven, or by simmering them in water to

Figure 19 Two methods of hooking wasp grubs

cook the insides to make them stay on the hook better. It is best, however, to use them in the natural state, and although you are bound to lose one or two off the hook at first, especially in fast water, with a little practice you will soon become proficient. Two recommended methods of hooking wasp grubs are illustrated in Figure 19.

The remainder, consisting of smaller, or misshapen grubs,

can be used as ground bait, but it is necessary first to drop them in water and remove and discard any that float.

WHEAT

A notable advantage in the use of creed wheat is that it is clean and pleasant to handle and needs very little preparation. It can also be bought prepared for use in sealed containers from the tackle dealers.

Creed wheat has been a noted bait for big roach for many years, especially where the river runs through industrial areas alongside grain wharves where wheat is continually falling into the water as the bags are being hoisted from the barges. In such areas huge shoals of roach congregate and acquire a definite liking for wheat.

Creeding Wheat

The method of preparing creed wheat is to wash the grain thoroughly and place it in a saucepan. Just cover with water and place the pan on the heat and slowly bring it to the boil. Allow it to simmer gently for an hour or two until the wheat swells in size and turns a golden brown, when the grain splits showing the white inside. It then has a frumenty smell and luscious look, and will be ready for use. A little sugar added before cooking helps to keep the wheat sweet and also promotes the browning. Some anglers prefer to stew their wheat in milk instead of water.

An alternative method of preparing wheat if you only need a small quantity is to put a tablespoonful of grain into a thermos flask and fill up with boiling water or milk, securing the cork and letting it stand all night. Next morning the grains will be fully creed ready for use.

Hooking Wheat

Short-shanked hooks seem to work best with wheat, just hooking the point through the white cooked kernel, protruding through the split. Be sure the point is brought right through again and is not covered in any way, to give the best possible chance of hooking fish (Figure 20).

Wheat is rather on the heavy side, which is a distinct advantage for it can be thrown a long way when distance is needed, and it also sinks straight to the bed of the swim. It is also very filling, so you must feed it into your swim very sparingly –

just a few grains little and often so as not to satisfy the fish.

The hook size favoured by many for wheat is a No 14 or a No 12. It is a first-class bait for roach and often produces some really big fish.

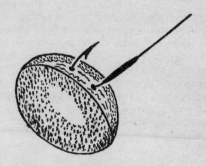

Figure 20 Insert hook point through white, cooked kernel protruding through split

PEARL BARLEY

Pearl barley is another good bait for most species of coarse fish, especially roach. It is prepared in the same way as wheat.

MISCELLANEOUS BAITS

This section deals with some baits that coarse fish have been known to take at one time or another. The list is not complete by any means and there are several other edible titbits which you will be able to add if you are one of those who likes to experiment.

Potatoes

Small potatoes, about the size of pigeons' eggs, lightly boiled and used on a hook of suitable size, make a good bait for carp and other bottom feeders when fished motionless on the bottom. Mashed potatoes, mixed up with a quantity of scalded bran, provides a very good groundbait, which is heavy and sinks quickly to the bottom. It is ideal for use in conjunction with hook baits of potato, bread or paste.

Meat
Pieces of cold meat fished on a large hook make a bait for barbel and chub. Groundbait with minced meat.

Sausage
Sections of raw sausage have proved killing baits for chub and barbel where the fish have become conditioned to them. This also applies to tinned meats – luncheon roll, etc.

Bacon
A piece of fat bacon seems to produce better results than the lean, for the latter often becomes too hard and brittle for the majority of fish to tackle. The inner rind of bacon also makes a good hook bait.

Beans
All types of beans, after being well cooked, will catch most coarse fish. Their advantage is that you can often purchase large quantities fairly cheaply, enabling you to bait your chosen swim lavishly, and so provide yourself with the probability of a good day's sport.

Peas
If you can secure a large quantity and cook them until tender they will probably ensure some really good sport if fed into the swim little and often.

Mussels
There are certain places, such as around the edges of a large weir pools, where freshwater mussels can be collected in fair quantities. Open the shells with a strong blade or screwdriver and scrape out all the soft insides into a bowl. Select a few of the large tongue-shaped pieces for hook baits and then chop up the rest for use as groundbait. The insides of saltwater mussels when well cooked can also be used in the same way.

Shrimps
Both freshwater and saltwater shrimps can be used for catching several species of coarse fish, especially barbel, bream and chub. After collecting them they should be well boiled and then peeled before use. Here again the best pieces are cut off for the hook with the remainder minced up for groundbait.

Macaroni
This is an excellent bait for chub, roach and dace. It is prepared by boiling in milk but must not be allowed to soften too much or it will not stay on the hook. Cut a few lengths about 1 in long for hook baits and then chop up the rest for groundbait.

Hips and Haws
These are used in their natural state when really ripe and soft. They will catch most species of coarse fish in their season, where the bushes overhang the water.

Elderberries
These can also be used in their natural state with one or two on the hook while others are pitched into the swim. Elderberries can be stored and preserved in glass jars for use when out of season. Wash them before placing them into the jars, cover with the preserving liquid and screw the lids on tightly. The usual preserving liquids are vinegar or formalin in the following proportions: one part of pure malt vinegar to three parts of water; or one part of formalin to ten parts of water.

Silkweed
This can be gathered from rocks and walls in a river, and is especially abundant below weirs. The weed is covered with minute crustaceans which are the main attraction to the fish. A small length of weed is wrapped round and round the hook to produce a ½-in diameter sphere, but still leaving the hook point bare. It is fished in the usual way. Many anglers prefer to draw a bare hook through the weed and use as bait the weed it collects – untouched by hand.

Currants and Sultanas
Rather expensive baits, but they will definitely catch fish when the swim is fed, again on the little and often principle, with a choice currant or sultana on the hook.

Cherries
These are used when really ripe and soft. Fished on the bottom for chub.

Bananas
Cut into slices ½ inch long and fish with a large hook on the bottom.

Caddis Grubs

These can be collected in the summer from the shallow edges of rivers and lakes. They can be seen crawling on the bottom or found under stones. They are covered with tiny sticks, stones or other debris, forming a tube or house in which they live. After collecting a good quantity, break open the cases and gently pull out the caddis grubs, or push them out with a matchstick, and store them in a tin containing damp moss. They are a deadly bait for roach and dace and should be hooked lightly through the tail. Caddis grubs can sometimes be bought at the aquarists' shops. They are the larvae of several species of sedge-fly.

Dock Grubs

All through the spring and summer dock grubs can be collected under the dock plants and flags which can be seen growing in their thousands along the river banks and hedgerows. When found growing in loose soil they can be easily pulled up and the grubs will be found among the roots. Fished on a large hook they are an excellent bait for chub, roach and dace.

Snails and Slugs

These can be collected at any time in wet weather and in the evenings and early mornings during dry spells. The snails are removed from their shells and are fished on a large hook on the bottom. The slugs are also fished on the bottom and they are reputed to have accounted for several large chub, carp, tench and bream.

Caterpillars

These are a natural bait for most species of fish, especially along the heavily wooded stretches where caterpillars are continually falling or being blown into the water. They are especially good for chub and dace. Here again, if you can collect them in sufficient quantities to feed your swim, little and often, you can expect some good sport.

Wood Lice and Earwigs

Both these creatures will catch roach and dace. They are usually fished by swimming the stream with float tackle. They can be collected by hanging old sacks in trees and on moist ground.

Grasshoppers and Cockchafers
Both these fairly large baits are reputed to have accounted for many big chub over the years. Useful as dapping baits.

Flies, Butterflies and Moths
All these will catch fish, especially chub and dace. They are usually fished on the surface. Dead bluebottles and green-bottles can be collected in large quantities if you save all your chrysalises. The flies can be killed with ammonia and when thrown on the water and allowed to float down the swim, the surface is very soon 'alive' with taking fish.

GROUNDBAITS

For successful coarse fish angling, you should always have a good stock of groundbait, kept dry in a large bin or tea chest.

Standard Groundbait
The most economical way to purchase groundbait is by the hundredweight bag, which will last for a very long time and works out cheaper than any you could make yourself. It can, of course, be bought in any smaller quantity. It is sold by nearly all fishing tackle dealers and can be bought by mail order from firms that advertise.

Preparation
You can prepare your own groundbait at home by spreading out slices of bread on newspapers in a warm room. When perfectly hard, pound and grind them up into powder. This is then riddled through the finest of sieves. One pound of semolina is added to every 5 lb of bread dust. This makes a perfect groundbait which only needs damping to the right consistency when you are about to go fishing.

The groundbait you purchase should also be passed through a very fine sieve to take out any large pieces. These can then be crushed to powder and passed through the sieve again, for ground bait must be as fine as possible, making sure it only whets the fishes' appetite and does not feed them. Here again you will improve the quality and efficiency if you add 1 lb of semolina to every 5 lb of groundbait, for the semolina acts as a binder and holds it together when pitching the com-pressed lumps containing your feeder maggots out to the re-quired spot.

When throwing groundbait always remember that the more accurate you become at hitting the exact spot every time, the more concentrated will be the fish below, making them, of course, all the easier to catch (Figure 21).

When you mix your groundbait be careful not to get it too wet or it will clog together and defeat the whole object of your riddling it to as fine a dust as possible, for you want it only to cloud the water and whet the fishes' appetites, not to feed them in any way.

'Wetting Up'

Place a couple of pounds of groundbait in a bowl and add a little lukewarm water at a time, stirring it in with a spoon. Then rub it up in your hands, making all the lumps fall away. In this way you can gradually damp it up to just the right consistency, which should be just wet enough for you to squeeze a handful tightly enough to stay in a lump for throwing, but which, on rubbing again in the hands, will immediately disintegrate without leaving any lumps at all.

Use of Milk

If you wet your groundbait with milk you will get a better clouding effect still, for milk is very penetrating in water and rapidly spreads over a wide area. This is a distinct advantage, especially in very clear, shallow water, for it helps to screen your movements from the fish.

Tinting Groundbaits

Groundbait can of course be tinted to any shade you fancy by adding a few drops of the colouring to the jug of damping liquid and stirring well before commencing to moisten the groundbait.

It is a good plan to have your groundbait tinted in colours that will contrast with your hook bait in order to show the latter off to advantage. If, say, you are using pink maggots on your hook, then a groundbait in a shade of yellow will make a good contrasting shade and show the hook baits off to their best advantage.

Dyes for tinting groundbait are the same as for tinting maggots and can be bought at most tackle dealers or by post.

The Swim-Feeder

Another method of groundbaiting is by the use of a gadget

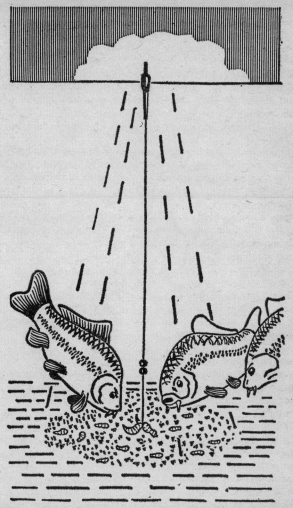

Figure 21 The more accurate you are at concentrating your groundbait into as small an area as possible, the easier the fish will be to catch

called a swim-feeder, consisting of a plastic or celluloid tube some 3 ins long and 1 inch in diameter, pierced all over with small holes. At each end, fine wire rings are fixed for its attachment to the line, usually just above the shots. The swim-feeder is packed with groundbait and maggots, and the angler casts his tackle out in the usual way.

The idea is that this method ensures that the groundbait will fall out very close to the hook bait, especially important in running water, and the makers claim that this method of groundbaiting is more accurate than pitching it in by hand in the usual way.

Amateurs have invented several types of swim-feeder and described them in the angling press. A popular basic form consists of the perforated cylindrical gadgets used by ladies for their hair-dressing, called 'rollers'. These can be bought quite cheaply in the stores.

Although the swim-feeder does put the groundbait in the right place, it takes quite a long time to get any quantity of groundbait down on to the bed of the swim owing to its very small capacity. Consequently, those anglers who can throw their groundbait in with a fair amount of accuracy can get on with the job of catching fish much more quickly than those who have to find time to keep on filling up the swim-feeder and making the repeated casts it requires.

Technique of Groundbaiting

When you reach your swim the first thing you should do is to study the water and choose the spot where you will place your float. Then throw in half a dozen handfuls of groundbait containing plenty of feeders or large maggots. This will settle on the river bed at the spot you have chosen and will probably collect a shoal of fish for you while you are assembling your tackle.

From then on you should feed your swim on the little and often principle, throwing in a small walnut-sized lump containing a few feeders about once every minute all the time you are fishing, in order to build up gradually a large shoal of fish. Then, according to the amount and size of fish you are catching, you can increase or decrease the size of your pieces.

Extra Ingredients

There are several ingredients which can be added to groundbait to make it more attractive. Egg shells finely broken up shine on the river bed and attract fish out of sheer curiosity.

Other ingredients are scalded bran, minced cabbage leaves and crushed cattle-cake. The groundbait can be damped up with blood, which is very good, especially for roach.

When groundbaiting in strong running water it is a good plan to mix in plenty of mashed potatoes. They are fairly heavy and help to take the groundbait down to the river bed more quickly.

Other Groundbaits

Bread dust is the generally accepted basic groundbait, but there are many other materials with which experiments can be made. A quantity of very light black loamy soil mixed with finely chopped red worms can be very deadly at times with bream, barbel and perch, when using a red worm on the hook.

Ledger Fishing

When ledger fishing it is a good idea to squeeze a good lump of groundbait tightly round the ledger. When you cast out and let it settle, the groundbait will be taken down to the river bed very close to the hook bait. Some anglers squeeze the ball of groundbait around the bait itself, especially when using a large bunch of maggots or a lob-worm. This is a really excellent method, for the feeding fish are quick to root into any large pieces of groundbait and soon find the bait inside and take it at once without suspicion. It is particularly useful in barbel fishing.

In Swift Water

One of the main points to watch when ground baiting your swim in running water is the accurate judgement of the speed of the water and the depth, for you must know where it is alighting on the river bed. In strong water you want it very heavy indeed and you may have to enclose it in a thin sphere of clay. Beware of the easiest of all mistakes to make, having your groundbait too light for the speed of water, for it will be swept away yards downstream and will never touch the bottom anywhere in your own swim and all your efforts will be a waste of time.

If you happen to make this mistake in an angling competition it is absolutely fatal to success, for you are then feeding for the competitors below you and handing them all your fish on a plate. Make sure that your groundbait is really heavy when fishing strong currents.

Emergency Groundbait

One of the easiest ways to make groundbait if you are in a hurry is simply to buy two or three loaves of bread, pull them into small pieces and place in a clean bag. This is then soaked at the waterside and the bread pulped up until it is of the right consistency for throwing into your swim.

Paper Bag Method

This method was often used in competitions during the last war when the use of bread groundbaits was banned. A pebble was put into each of a number of small paper bags together with a few maggots, and the tops screwed up. A bag was pitched out to the required spot, and the water-soaked bag would burst when it reached the bed of the swim.

Another effective groundbait can be made by damping three or four separate bowlfuls of groundbait, each one being tinted in a different colour. When mixed together the multi-coloured effect makes a very attractive groundbait.

For most species of fish it is advisable to groundbait every minute or so. Carp and tench are exceptions. Once a good carpet of groundbait has been laid down nothing should be done to disturb the water for these shy fish.

FLAVOURINGS

For hundreds of years anglers of all nationalities have been searching for an elusive dope that will make fish mad with hunger and also attract them into the swim from great distances. Whether or not one day some lucky angler will stumble across a dope to beat all dopes remains to be seen, but some flavourings attract fish – naturally enough when it is remembered that a fish's sense of smell and taste is very highly developed, especially among the bottom feeders such as barbel, carp, tench and bream.

It is a well-known fact that salmon roe is a most deadly bait and its peculiar smell penetrates very quickly through water and is known to attract fish lying downstream from great distances. Salmon roe proved so irresistible that its use as bait is forbidden by statute, as is all other roe.

It is also claimed that blood, aniseed or linseed, when used in the ground bait, gives the angler a decided advantage and definitely helps him to catch more fish.

Scientists have proved that fish can smell and taste much better than they can see, and an American firm has produced an ointment (sold in tubes like toothpaste) which, it is claimed, has an irresistible smell for fish and brings them fighting round the anglers' hooks. The ointment is called 'Strike', and is made from clams and horse liver.

In France there is a similar dope, also put up in tubes. It is produced in a variety of colours, and smells of aniseed and mint. Many French anglers on the River Seine are making big claims for it.

Also from America is the Gipsey Fish Bait Oil which smells like linseed oil and, according to the testimonials which have appeared in the makers' advertisements from time to time, it has produced some tremendous catches of fish both in fresh water and in salt water.

Because the senses of smell and taste in fish are so highly developed, especially among the bottom feeders, it may be worthwhile to experiment with different dopes on your own waters, for one particular flavouring may go well in one place and not in another and *vice versa*.

The following is a list of dopes and flavourings available to the angler. They can be obtained in chemists' shops, and in the bigger tackle shops. They are advertised in the angling press.

Spike Lavender Oil	Verbena Oil
Oil of Fennel	Cummin Oil
Oil of Rhodium	Aniseed Oil
Aniseed Powder	Pilchard Oil

DYES

Although it may be argued that the colouring of baits and groundbaits is of little use when fishing deep-coloured waters for bream and barbel, which in those conditions rely on their sense of smell to find their food, it is a different story when fishing in very clear and fairly shallow water for the keen-sighted roach and dace. In these conditions it is worthwhile to make your hook baits and groundbaits as attractive as possible.

There is a long list of maggot dyes on the market and a

number of powders for colour feeding available to those anglers who prefer to breed their own bait. With a little ingenuity and patience it is possible to get a wide range of colours.

Yellow and Orange

Probably the most useful dye powders are chrysiodine and chrysiodine R. Very little is needed to give your maggots brilliant shades of yellow and orange according to the make and strength of the powders which give all shades from bright yellow to deep rose.

Maggots should always be well scoured and cleaned before attempting to dye them for any grease on their bodies prevents the dye from taking. An easy way with chrysiodine powder is to empty the maggots into a bowl-shaped sieve with a handle and first give them a thorough washing under the cold-water tap. Then sprinkle on a small quantity of dye powder and shake gently. Keep on shaking them until all are well coloured and the shade is rather darker than you want it. Rinse well under the cold-water tap again. Dry them off and place in a clean tin.

Pink and Red

To colour maggots pink and red you will need rhodamine powder. After washing the maggots under the cold-water tap place them in a tin and sprinkle on a good quantity of rhodamine. Replace the lid and put them in a warm place for a couple of hours at least, for it takes much longer to get a really bright shade of pink than it does to produce the yellow shades with chrysiodine.

Colour Feeding

The best way to colour maggots is to colour feed them on the meat when the colours go right inside them and are permanent and translucent. The powder is sprinkled on the meat as soon as the eggs have appeared and the tiny maggots take in the colour with the meat right from birth. A well-known colour feed for shades of yellow is annatto roll, commerically used for colouring butter.

Do not dye your hook baits too dark. Remember the light, bright shades are the most attractive, especially if the swim is deep and the light not too good.

Your groundbaits, too, can be tinted to any shade you

desire and it is a sound plan to have your hook baits and groundbaits in two contrasting colours so one is showing off the other to the best advantage.

Most leading fishing tackle dealers carry a stock of dyes. If there is any difficulty they can be bought from advertisers in the angling press.

The following is a list of dyes in general use:

Bismarck Brown.
Rhodamine B. (Rose).
Chrysiodine (Orange Yellow).
Chrysiodine R. (Orange Red).
Methyl Violet (Milk White).
Auromine O. (Lemon Yellow).
Methylene Blue.
Eosine (Red).
Brilliant Green (Pale Green).
Malachite Green (Pale Green).
Fluorescene (Mustard Yellow).
Chrysiodine 3R. (Hot Orange).
Rhodamine B.N. (Deep Rose).
Annatto Roll, for colour feeding maggots and
    feeders (Yellow).
Methylene Blue mixed with varying proportions
    of Auromine O. gives a range of greens.
A mixture of Chrysiodine and Rhodium B.
    produces a deep salmon-pink colour.

FISH AND BAITS

In the following list the most important baits are shown in SMALL CAPITALS:

Barbel. LOBWORMS, MAGGOTS, CHEESE and CHEESE PASTES. Barbel have been caught on almost every recognized bait – including small live bait early in the season – and on many freak ones.

Bleak. MAGGOTS, PASTES, SCRAPS OF WORM.

Bream. WORMS OF ALL KINDS, MAGGOTS, HEMP SEED, BREAD and BREAD PASTES, wheat, wasp grubs.

Carp. BREAD and BREAD PASTES (white or brown, plain or flavoured with honey or sugar), LOBWORMS, PARBOILED

POTATOES, other worms, bloodworms, maggots, grubs of all kinds, wheat, leguminous vegetables.

Chub. CHEESE and CHEESE PASTES, WORMS, MAGGOTS, LARGE FLIES, CATERPILLARS AND SIMILAR INSECTS, ELDERBERRIES, CHERRIES. Chub are the most omnivorous of freshwater fish and anything edible, of suitable size, is likely to be taken.

Crucian carp. MAGGOTS, BREAD and BREAD PASTES, SMALL WORMS.

Dace. MAGGOTS, SMALL WORMS, BREAD and BREAD PASTES, HEMP SEED, freshwater shrimps and molluscs, grubs, etc.

Eels. LARGE WORMS, FRESH DEAD FISH. Any 'meat' bait.

Gudgeon. MAGGOTS, SMALL WORMS, BLOODWORMS, PASTES.

Perch. WORMS, SMALL LIVE BAIT, PLUGS AND SPINNERS, maggots, small frogs, grubs, etc.

Pike. LIVE BAIT, DEAD FISH INCLUDING SPRATS AND HERRINGS, PLUGS AND SPINNERS, worms, frogs and other 'meat' baits.

Roach. MAGGOTS, BREAD and PASTES, HEMP SEED, small worms, grubs of all kinds, fresh water shrimps and small molluscs, earwigs, wood lice, etc.

Rudd. RED WORMS, MAGGOTS, BREAD and BREAD PASTES, any type of grub or small insect.

Tench. LOBWORMS, BREAD AND BREAD PASTES, freshwater mussels, snails and other molluscs, parboiled potatoes.

Roach

(See Figure 67, page 214)

DESCRIPTION

The Roach (*Rutilus rutilus*) is a member of the carp family – (*Cyprinidae*) and is one of the commonest of freshwater fishes. It is generally distributed throughout England and Wales, but is absent from northern Scotland and Ireland. In most parts of Cornwall, Devon and West Wales it is rare.

The general appearance of roach is as follows: the body is deep and compressed; its depth about one-third of the total length, without caudal fin; mouth terminal; the upper jaw but slightly projecting beyond the lower. There are three longitudinal series of scales between the lateral line and ventral fin. Origin of the dorsal fin above, but not in advance of the root of the ventral.

The colour of the upper parts is dusky green with blue reflections, becoming lighter on the sides and passing into silvery white on the belly. The iris is bright red, the cheeks and gill-covers silvery white. The dorsal and caudal fins are pale brown, the pectorals orange-red, the ventrals and anal bright red. The colour scheme varies according to the locality and type of water from which they come.

The position of the dorsal fin in relation to the ventral will at once distinguish the roach from the rudd; in the former the origin of the dorsal is only slightly behind that of the ventral. In the latter it is conspicuously so (see Figure 67).

River roach are as a rule most handsome fish, and generally much darker in appearance than those caught in ponds and lakes, and the fins are much brighter. They have a bronze appearance similar to chub, which seems to fade away some hours after capture. Roach spawn from April to May, if weather conditions and water temperature are normal for the time of year; cold weather and lack of sunshine retard the process, whereas fine warm weather with a high water temperature will speed it up.

GROWTH

The growth of roach, as with all other species of fish, is governed by the amount of food available, plus the environment. If the conditions in which they live are good and suitable, they will put on weight in a normal manner; on the other hand their growth will be retarded if food is scarce and surroundings bad.

On many waters, especially lakes and ponds, undersized fish are common, and as the years go by this state of affairs gets worse and worse. Roach multiply each season by many thousands, and the time eventually comes when a lake or pond with sufficient food to maintain, say, 20,000 fish, has to maintain 100,000. It is obvious, therefore, that growth is bound to be retarded, and the fish eventually become dwarfs.

The growth of roach under normal conditions is rather slow during the first two or three years, attaining a length of only 4 to 5 ins, but after this it increases more rapidly.

The average life-span of roach is eight years, when they can weigh anything from 8 oz to 2 lb or more, according to the conditions under which they live.

HABITAT

Subject to the wide distribution mentioned above, roach can be found in almost every type of fresh water that can support fish life except shallow mountain streams. They are gregarious by nature, and I have found that shoals generally consist of roach of approximately the same size. This is very noticeable on the Hampshire Avon, a river which I know particularly well. On many occasions I have had good bags of roach all of about 1 lb; on others, fish of 1½ lb; and on two occasions a bag of seven roach all of which were over 2 lb – with no fish of smaller size taken.

HYBRIDS

During the past twenty years many roach-bream hybrids have been recorded as true roach, and it is very necessary therefore that the angler should be able to determine the difference for himself.

Here, then, are the distinguishing marks between the true roach, hybrids and bream.

True Roach
The number of rays in the pectoral fin is 16, in that of the ventral fin 9 or 10, those of the anal fin 9-11, the dorsal fin 9-11, and last, the caudal fin which has 19 rays.

Hybrid Roach-Bream
Pectoral fin 16 rays, ventral fin 9, anal fin 15-20, dorsal fin 10 and caudal fin 17 rays.

Bream
The pectoral fin 16 rays, the ventral fin 10, anal fin 24-30, dorsal fin 8 to 10 and the caudal fin 30 rays.

The dorsal fin of a true roach is placed almost directly in line over the ventral fin, whereas the dorsal fin of both the roach-bream hybrid and that of the rudd is set much nearer the tail or caudal fin.

Although the number of 2-lb roach and over caught during the past fifty years must now run into several thousands, I still consider a 2-lb roach a fine specimen. Fifty years ago a 2-lb roach was looked upon as a rarity by the average club angler, but I doubt very much if they were really rare.

ADVICE TO BEGINNERS

For those about to take up roach fishing a few words about how to make a start will not be out of place. Fortunate is the man who starts under the guidance of a skilled angler, for he picks up the ABC of the game unconsciously. Less fortunate ones, without this grounding, may muddle along for years.

The rod is important, and the ideal thing is to go out with angling friends and try rods until you find one that suits you. Weight and length are important factors, coupled with the question of cost. Select a rod that is comfortable to use.

I recommend that the beginner starts with a Nottingham type reel – ie the centre pin or revolving drum type. Fixed spool reels are excellent, but they are best left alone until general experience has been gained.

Now we come to the smaller items such as lines, floats, hooks, etc, and my advice to the beginner is to copy your friends to start off with; but I shall deal with them more fully as I go along.

Compact Equipment
It has always appealed to me to have a well-arranged compact fishing equipment. Many anglers pay too little attention to this. There should be 'a place for everything, and everything in its place'. Consider: the time saved, accessibility, comfort in travelling, ease and quickness of assembling and dismantling, changing from one style of fishing to another, moving from place to place, etc. I therefore offer a few hints and suggestions as to how this can be accomplished.

Rods
Never carry more than you actually need for the day's fishing, making two the limit. I try to stick to one.

On the rod bag you use most, sew a pocket (on the bottom outside end) large enough to take your landing net handle, rod rests and landing net (the type of net which, when folded up, lies parallel with the rods). Then have an extra tape sewn approximately 18 ins from the bottom to keep these items in position. There is now no fear of losing them, and there is the added advantage that your net is not taking up room in your basket.

Bag, Basket or Box
I vote for the basket every time; it is light, makes an excellent seat, and everything inside is accessible.

Winders
These should be single ones. Multiple winders are a curse, for with them tangles are frequent and often prevent a quick change-over. But that is not all. To have half a dozen lines made up is bad practice, for hooks go rusty and the gut is exposed to light and heat and gradually gets weaker. With nylon monofilament this does not apply.

So use single winders. Three for your float lines, if you must have so many, one for each light, medium and heavy floats. Should you need more, I recommend the following: obtain some small barrel leads or half-moon leads, and test half a dozen floats at home; attach the requisite amount of lead to each float with a piece of thread and carry them in your basket this way. Making up a float line now can be done

68

in double quick time, and in addition, you have a perfectly reliable hook and cast, and you also save space by doing away with the big multiple winder.

Baits
One should have special containers of the right size for all baits. For maggots a wide shallow plastic container is best, so that the maggots can be picked up easily, and time is saved in rebaiting. Deep tins, liable to rust, are not recommended.

When using maggots on a winter's day, a small container should also be carried; into this put a few dozen maggots and slip it into your trousers pocket. You will then have some nice lively fellows for hook bait, all dancing for joy!

Casts and Hooks
These should be kept in a wallet. Each packet in this container should be plainly marked, and on no account should odds and ends be put into it.

Keep Net
This should be dressed and on the large side, with a good stout cord – not string – attached. To the end of this cord tie a meat skewer.

Rod Rests
These should be 3 ft in length, short ones being useless in soft ground. Made to this length they pack up so much better with your rods. Paint them white, otherwise you may leave them behind when you pack up fishing for the day.

Plummet and Disgorger
Carry these in one of your pockets; do not throw them into your basket for valuable time is lost if you do.

Pliers
This item can be left loose in the bottom of your basket. Other small items such as lead wire, barrel leads, shots, etc, can be carried in a small box or bag, but do not get into the habit of carrying everything in boxes.

I never carry even the most expensive reel covered, for when I get back at night I am reminded that the reel must be cleaned and the line dried. However, that is a matter of choice.

Arrange your kit in really good style. Not only will it be a pleasure for life, it will be a means of catching more trains and more fish than otherwise you would have done; moving from spot to spot along the river banks will be a pleasure instead of a tiresome necessity, and packing up will be – as it should be – done inside two minutes.

One Rod Only

What a mistake it is to fish with more than one rod at a time! There are exceptions, of course, as when pike disturb the swim, but as a general rule one rod only should be used. Many a day's fishing has been spoiled by anglers who try to fish with two – for they cannot concentrate on either.

Concentration and perseverance on one style of fishing at a time must be the aim of the novice; it is so with the expert, and if the experts cannot manage two rods, it is very certain that novices cannot.

Again there are anglers who spoil their day's fishing by attempting too many things. They start off perhaps with a spot of roaching, and before their groundbait has had time to do its job they pack up and try spinning. Fed up with this after a short while they turn to roaching again, and in addition put out a live bait. In a very short time they decide to try another swim ... and so it goes on throughout the day, no one style or swim being thoroughly tried out.

There are others who must have a ledger going at the same time as swimming for roach. One may catch a fish now and again on this ledger by accident or otherwise, but it is a bad practice.

Try to cultivate a better procedure for the day; try to determine the best thing to do, and having decided, go full out for an hour or so, and concentrate and persevere on this and this alone.

It is very difficult, if not impossible, to determine, prior to leaving home, which swim to fish or which style to employ, because on arrival you may find a strong north-east wind, the water temperature may be too low for roaching or there may be other drawbacks. The answer to this is – never be in too great a hurry to start fishing. Weigh up everything before unpacking, and defeat the wind if you possibly can; for a 'Jack in the box' float will drive the fish away. Study everything well, and having decided on where to go and what to fish for, stick to it – and with one rod only.

Plumbing the Depth

The majority of anglers, both young and old, are in too great a hurry to start fishing. This is a mistake, for a few minutes spent on this most important job of plumbing can make all the difference to a day's fishing. Correct plumbing is, in my opinion, the second most important matter in connection with our hobby (groundbaiting taking first place), and it should be done intelligently and with care.

Time and again it has occurred to me how few the anglers are who pay sufficient attention to plumbing the depth. The average angler is content to plumb immediately in front of him and then start fishing. This may be quite all right sometimes, but it is often entirely wrong.

All anglers of experience know that at a certain spot in a swim you get most bites. The reason for this is that fish have a particular spot in the river no matter where they may be, both for feeding and living. The spot for feeding in the case of coarse fish is invariably a clean patch or run. The swim you are fishing may have only one such spot over its whole length, or there may be a shelf where the fish know food collects. It is at these spots where food collects that you get most of your bites, no matter whether you yourself have attracted the fish to the swim, or whether you are fishing a well-known and well-used swim. There are noted swims – and surely there is a reason why fish continually inhabit such places.

Take the case of two anglers fishing from a punt, their respective floats not more than 2 ft apart, one angler getting all the fish; the other, not a bite. I have actually inspected the bottom afterwards, and seen the reason. In one case I found the nature of the bottom in front of the two anglers entirely different; in front of one, small gravel; in front of the other, fairly big stones and cobbles, and the fish were feeding on the fine or small gravel. On other occasions it has been due to something entirely different, such as a dirty bottom in front of one, and a clean run in front of the other.

At other times I have found the cause to be the drift of the groundbait, the majority of which had come to rest at one particular spot, the result being that one man got the bulk of the sport, and the other looked on in amazement.

Even in ponds, lakes and reservoirs, where the bottom is often foul, there are spots where fish feed more freely than in others; this is entirely due to the surroundings, and the nature of the bottom.

These spots are much more difficult to find than in river fishing.

It pays every time to ascertain the nature of the bottom, and to find out as much as you possible can *before* commencing to fish, for you then know exactly where to position yourself, and more important still, where to put your groundbait.

I cannot emphasize too strongly the value of plumbing the depth. Plumb here, plumb there, plumb everywhere. You are unlikely to frighten the fish away, and even if you do they will come back again.

So in future when you arrive at a swim that you do not know, plumb the depth in front of you (as in common practice) and then in two or three places to your left and two or three to your right; also nearer to you and farther out than you normally fish. You may find the water on your right slightly deeper than in front of you, and the same on your left; this means, of course, that there is a slight rise in the bed of the river immediately in front of you. In most cases this swim should be fished with the high ground at the tail-end of the swim for it acts as a trap for the food, and fish know that, so position yourself accordingly. There are other points to remember. It is far better to have your fish collect well away from you than immediately in front – the flash of your rod in casting, the disturbance when landing a fish – these factors are very important, especially when the water is shallow and clear. Even though the rise in the river bed be only a matter of inches, take advantage of it.

In another spot you find there is a hole, and it may extend some distance; if it does, give it a trial, more especially in winter. The hole you find in another spot may be only a small one, extending not more than a few feet, and perhaps there may be some stream – however, fish it. Plumb the depth of the hole and throw your line upstream, holding it back and easing it down until you reach (or just before you reach) the hole, then let it go and swim the hole; many a nice fish I have had in holes only a few feet in length.

In other swims you find that by casting out a little farther or nearer the bank the water deepens; here again is a spot worth trying.

Always use a heavy plummet. It is of great value in ascertaining the true nature of the bottom. One can tell whether there is mud, sand, shingle, or large stones, weed, etc, with a little practice, and that is almost impossible with a very small plummet, especially if there is much stream running.

In a river or anywhere where there is a stream running small shingle is decidedly the best bottom. Sand comes next, large gravel takes third place, weeds come next and mud last. One should never fish over mud if it can possibly be avoided when there is a stream running; in still water it is somewhat different for the species differ: they have different surroundings and habits. Some prefer a soft mud or silt bottom, others a hard one. However, as a general rule for river fishing, find the hard bottom every time, and you can tell immediately if your plummet is heavy enough.

Some swims you find will have very uneven bottoms; these as a rule do not produce the best results. Other swims where a shelf exists (a sudden drop of a foot or more) are as a rule very good; the shelf acts as a trap for food and also gives cover to the fish, both from the sun and their enemies, according to position.

Again, in a swim that you find deepens considerably as it nears the bank, try the happy medium. Do not fish your usual distance out, for there is a reason for the water becoming deeper. It shows that when a push of water is on it flows towards the bank slightly, bringing food with it. Stand back and fish a few feet from the bank first, and if nothing is doing, try a little farther out.

On the other hand, in swims that you find deepen the farther you go from the bank, try fishing out as far as you can, for here is the natural channel, where the majority of food rolls along, where fish seek it, and, above all, where the bottom is cleanest.

Now we come to the most tiresome of all swims; you plumb the depth, and wherever you go you find weed. However, keep on plumbing, for eventually you will find a patch which is clean, perhaps only a few feet in length, perhaps long enough to swim. In either case fish it, either by laying on, with crust or paste, in the small patch, or by swimming it if it is long enough.

Never put a shot on your hook length when fishing near or through weeds, for its progress is much more natural without one, and in addition the chances of getting caught up are much less, because it is carried with and deviates with the slightest variation of the current. I strongly advise anglers never to use a shot on the hook length, my long experience having taught me that it pays to do without one even when breadcrust fishing in fast water.

In all the various items mentioned (and remember it applies to all of them) never be content to let your depth remain constant the whole time you are fishing if fish are few and far between. Adding or dropping a few inches may make all the difference; and many and many a time I have made a slight alteration in my depth and got fish straight away.

In swims you wish to fish which are too far out to plumb,

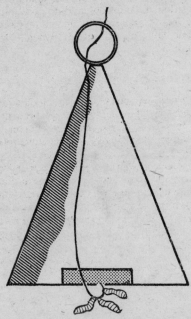

Figure 22 A small cork inset holds the hook firmly without danger to the point

plumb as far out as you possibly can, and then boldly add a foot or more and keep on adding if necessary until you start to drag. Then correct. It is on most occasions better to be too deep than not deep enough.

A word on the plummet itself. Use a big one, even in sluggish or deep water, for it is of far greater importance to know the exact nature of the bottom you are going to fish over than is the fear of frightening the fish away. Fish cannot differentiate between a 1-oz and 2-oz lead so get one of 2 oz. I always carry a 2-oz plummet.

Do not pick your plummet straight up and out of the water if you have any doubts as to the nature of the bottom. Try gently dragging it along a few inches. This will save time and precious groundbait very often.

Another point about the plummet – make the ring much bigger than it usually is, for you often may wish to correct your depth when you have a beautiful bunch of maggots or a nice tail-end of lob on your hook and do not wish to interfere with it. If the ring is large enough, you can pass the whole lot through, plumb your depth and be fishing again in a few seconds (Figure 22).

BAITS AND GROUNDBAITS

(Capt. Parker's original book contained a long section on baits and groundbaits. As these subjects have been dealt with in general, and at length, in the previous chapter, we include here only matters particularly concerning roach fishing. [Ed.])

When after roach in a river, my procedure has always been to try breadcrust or flake first. If there is nothing doing, I change to maggots, and keep on changing until the last hour, when I change to crust and stick to it until it is time to pack up. This procedure has stood me in good stead in most places, especially in winter fishing when you find the water clear with a low temperature.

I shall not go too deeply into the question of the hook sizes to use because it must vary with the size of bait used, and also the type of water fished, but when using crust and maggots alternately, I strike a medium and use size 9 or 10. When using crust in winter I invariably use size 8.

For still-water roach fishing in summer, things are vastly different.

The favourite bait for a particular water may be one of many – wheat, paste, crust, maggots, worms, etc. Here again the hook size may vary.

If using single maggot, then any size from 12 to 18 will suffice, size 12 being good for most baits with the exception of crust.

The size of maggot to use has always been a controversial

subject especially among the experts, so I shall speak only of my experience with them.

Large maggots are favoured by many, especially those who wish to fish with single maggot, for it saves time, a very important matter when match fishing. Leaving match fishing out of the question, I do not like large maggots, for they die quickly and then hang on the hook like a piece of wet string. On the other hand if you are prepared to bait up much more frequently, and you are fishing sluggish or still water, I see nothing against them. But if fishing fast-running water I avoid using them if I can; bringing them back against fast water kills them almost immediately.

My experience has been that the average size maggot is far and away the best, and I much prefer two of these to one large one, for they live much longer, are more attractive because of two wriggles instead of one and fewer bites are missing owing to their shorter length.

Paste

This is a very good bait indeed for roach, either for swimming or ledgering, but it must be made on the soft side, hard paste being useless. Many anglers spoil their chances by making their paste too hard. 'It stops on so much longer,' they say. It certainly stays on longer, but roach do not like hard baits, and I have seen them eject it like a shot from a gun. Make the paste as soft as conditions will permit; it is far better to bait up frequently, and catch fish, than it is to bait up at long intervals and catch none.

Hemp Seed

This is a wonderful bait, but I do not recommend it for general use when roach fishing; it will, of course, catch fish galore on some waters, but not on all. Even on Father Thames, where it was introduced, I have caught many more roach on crust than I have on hemp. On the other hand many more fish will be caught on some stretches of the Thames and other waters, when using hemp, than when using maggots or any other bait.

Experience alone, both personal and local, can guide you in this respect.

Elderberries

A very popular bait on waters where hemp seed is used.

Wheat

This is a very good bait indeed on some waters, especially canals, lakes, gravel pits and ponds, and it is favoured by many. In fact it will catch roach almost anywhere, including fast-running rivers, but it is not used generally in fast water. My own experience has been that even on a water where wheat is common bait, ordinary soft bread paste has been the most killing for roach. On the same water I found wheat best for bream; again showing the importance of changing the bait occasionally unless you know the water well.

Groundbaits

Now we come to the very secret of success, for no matter what type of water you may be fishing, it is groundbaiting a swim correctly that counts. If only anglers would give more care, thought and patience both to its preparation and use, then bags would be increased tenfold.

The most important thing is to know exactly what your groundbait is doing as it lies on the river bed, whether it is in the correct position, or rolling along instead of remaining put. Is it disintegrating too fast or too slow? etc.

Preparing the Groundbait

A really first-class preparation can be made from bread alone. This I have found is equally effective on both still and fast-running waters, provided it is made up to the right consistency. I have been using it now for many seasons, and have no desire to change at all.

Stale bread is best, and should be put in soak overnight, or some few hours before making – first cutting it into thick slices.

When ready, you wring as much water as possible from each slice and throw it into a bucket. You start pounding it with your fist, and keep going for several minutes until it is kneaded into a paste. If you have made it too stiff, it can be broken down by adding a little water. If it is too soft, you must mix some dry bread with it.

The effectiveness of groundbait must depend on how it disintegrates when in the water. If it is made to the consistency of paste as ordinarily used for hook bait, it is useless, and if made too soft it is washed away downstream much too quickly.

Many anglers put their faith in maggots as groundbait for

attracting fish to their swim no matter what water they are fishing, and a very attractive method it is too; but I do not recommend it unless you are a very experienced angler, my reasons being: the head of fish in a particular place may be very small, in which case the fish would soon satisfy their appetites and stop feeding, but you would still continue to throw them in from time to time, whereas the cloud ground bait gives them practically nothing to feed on, as the particles are so minute.

Reading a Water

The ability to read a water can add immeasurably to both pleasure and the chances of catching fish. It is advisable to cultivate this habit and to develop it. Imagine the joy it would bring to be able to stroll along a river, stream or lake and be able to read it, ie, to be able to know within certain limits the spots where fish are likely to be, and in many cases be able to determine the species of fish most likely to be there.

All species of fish like a certain environment, for what suits one does not suit another. Some of our lakes, for instance, are noted for carp or tench; others for pike or bream; while others are good for roach, perch and so on. The same applies on rivers where many different species exist: some like the deeps, others the fast-running shallows, while others prefer the slack water, etc.

The preferences of fish for various strengths of stream can, I think, be divided into three groups:

(1) Trout, grayling, barbel and dace like a good fast stream.

(2) Roach, chub, pike, perch and gudgeon prefer the more sluggish parts of the river.

(3) Carp, tench, bream and rudd are in their element in still water, although some of these species inhabit certain rivers.

Pike and perch live near rush and reed beds. Chub can be found in both deep and shallow water provided it is slack; their favourite haunts being eddies, deep and shallow holes near the bank if there is a fast water near at hand, which can bring a good supply of food to them.

The first consideration is food. Without it, fish cannot live, so it is only natural that their animal instincts tell them where to find it.

In rivers one must study the course of the stream. If it runs into the bank, one can assume that it brings food with it. Watch the debris as it floats down, or the flies when they are on the water.

In the case of the roach fisherman the same applies, but at the same time you must consider the time of the season and the conditions prevailing. If the stream brings food in a certain direction on the surface, why should it not bring food in the same direction on the bottom? This is exactly what does happen, so it is up to you to find such a spot and position yourself accordingly.

What happens is this. During the flood periods when the speed of the stream is perhaps double or treble its normal speed, it scours the bed of the river and makes channels or corrugations into which the food is carried down. And the fish know it.

To find these channels, one has to plumb most carefully, and groundbait likewise, because it is here that you want your hook bait to travel. If there is a gradual rise in the river bed, position yourself so that the rise is at the end of the swim or nearly so.

In addition to this, the channels are the cleanest spots, and feeding fish, especially roach, like the clean patches on the river bed.

As I have already stated, one must take prevailing conditions into consideration, so we will assume that the river is in spate. It is now that you have to put on your thinking cap.

If the spate is, say, one day old, the stream will perhaps be very muddy and bring with it a lot of rubbish. This makes the fish sick and they retire to the slack water. If the spate continues, the fish become really ill, and not only lose their appetite, but all colour goes from their fins and they look very anaemic indeed.

Some of the fish find their way on such occasions to parts that are not affected by the stream, and to where the water is shallow because it is here that the water is not so coloured and they can see their food. Here then is the place to fish.

When the water starts to fine down, the fish will gradually

recover from their sickness, but they are not strong enough yet to face the full force of the current. So the places to fish are those where the stream is steady, such as eddies, near bends in the river, and at the mouth of dykes.

The next step is when the water has returned almost to normal and has fined down sufficiently for the fish to see their food in any part of the river. It is now that you must make no mistake as to where to fish, because they have recovered from their sickness and are hungry after perhaps a long fast. At periods like this the fish go in search of food and can be had in fast shallow water. Often I have caught them on ledger tackle, knowing that to attempt float fishing would be out of the question.

At other times we find different conditions altogether. Hard frosts have set in, the water temperature is very low, the wind is strong. This again calls for careful thought before hurrying to get your line in the water. The fish become lethargic on such occasions, and in consequence go to spots where the stream is more sluggish and where they can rest. But it does not always mean that the fish are disinclined to feed. It does on occasions when the water temperature has dropped suddenly or fallen to 5°C (40°F) or below. There is only one thing to do in these circumstances when after roach — go searching. Search for a spot out of the wind, one that has deep water for preference, and where there is little stream. Actually, it is a day to go chubbing or piking when conditions are like this. If you go chubbing or roaching, ledgering is much better than swimming the bait.

On the next occasion when you go fishing you may find a different set of conditions altogether. You arrive at the water to find the sun right at your back, the water gin clear, together with a wind in your face, three things most of us dislike. This again means you must go searching, for you do not want your shadow on the water. The wind, too, is in your face, making casting more difficult, and this means that many more shadows are falling on the water and on the bed of the river in your efforts to get line out.

These matters must be taken into consideration if you wish to read a water, and locate a swim. Do not take the view that life is too short to bother with them – it is fish you are after, with contentment at the end of the day, and both can be gained by the expenditure of a few moments' thought prior to starting to fish.

SHADOWS

I do not think we pay sufficient attention to shadows. We all know they scare the fish, but in our keenness to start fishing we just forget. The fly fisherman is much more careful in this respect than the average bottom angler, probably because he is so much more active, travelling up and down continuously wielding his rod.

Every angler knows that he must not position himself with the sun behind him, casting his shadow in a great patch in front of him where he wants to fish. This he knows will scare the fish, and if he is fishing a stream with his shadow continually moving, it makes matters much worse. But it is of errors less obvious than this that I am now writing.

From time to time I have studied the lesser shadows carefully through my water telescope, and I am convinced they are often the cause of a blank morning or afternoon's fishing. Even a fine-running line casts a thick shadow on the river bed, and much more so does a float and rod.

Further, these shadows alter in size according to the position of the sun in relation to the equipment; when the sun is immediately overhead the shadows are smallest, and as the sun declines in the heavens, the shadows grow bigger.

With a little thought you can avoid these most detrimental shadows. I will illustrate my meaning with three imaginary instances (Figure 23). Supposing that you are fishing and facing a stream with the sun on your own side of the stream more or less behind you, and the water flowing away from your right hand side towards your left.

A. – If the sun behind you is somewhat to your left, throwing your shadow upstream, the tail of your swim is the end to fish, and in consequence your groundbait should be settled there, not in front of you or upstream; concentrate your efforts in that direction, pay out line, and fish farther downstream than you normally do. The position of your groundbait is the important item; if it is placed in front of or above you, the fish will head up to it into your moving shadows which will scare them away.

B. – If the sun behind is on your right it becomes more difficult to avoid your shadows falling on your swim as they are now thrown downstream to your left. So instead of fishing your normal distance from the bank, increase the length of your line enough to allow the hook bait to travel down say, ten

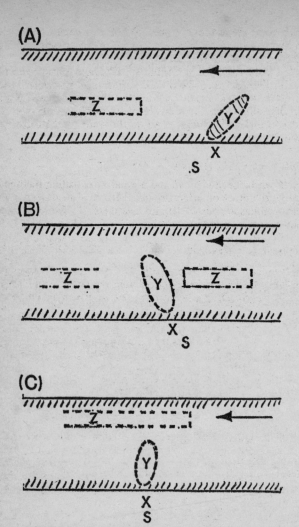

Figure 23 X = Angler and rod. Y = Shadow area. Z = Best fishing area. S = Sun. Arrow indicates direction of current

feet beyond the shadow of your rod on the water. This time
see that your ground bait settles well upstream and fish as
much as possible in that direction.

C. – If the sun is right behind you take note of the position
and distance of your shadows as they fall on the water, and
fish as far as you possibly can beyond them. The ideal position of course is to have the sun more or less facing you so
that you make no shadow at all on the water; but this is not
always possible.

SPECIAL METHODS

Roach can be caught by all the normal float fishing methods
and by all forms of ledgering (see Figures 5 to 9), but two
other methods are worth detailed treatment. They are using a
wooden ledger; and long-trotting.

WOODEN LEDGER

My favourite method when fishing for roach in still water is
as follows: make a wooden ledger approximately ½ inch by ¾
inch in length. Drill a hole in the centre, run it down your

Figure 24 The wooden ledger for still water fishing

cast on to a shot, then place another shot on the other end.
Your wooden ledger is now a fixture. Now add a shot or two
at either end until the ledger is submerged, or practically level
with the surface of the water, the idea being that with the
added weight of bait and cast the ledger will very gradually
sink to the bottom (Figure 24).

Now try to imagine what happens when you have a bite and
the fish moves off. Owing to the fact that the fish carries the
weight of your bait, the ledger will have a tendency to rise and
by so doing all drag is eliminated.

And now to the question of casting a long distance. All that
is necessary is to squeeze groundbait round the wooden

ledger, and when making the cast, aim high so that the groundbait will break up on impact with the water. If you make the ground bait to the right consistency and it breaks up on striking the water, it is not only distributed better, but it permits your ledger to sink very slowly to the bottom. Again, you may have a bite soon after your bait comes to rest, in which case you have no ground bait adhering to the ledger, and everything is free for the fish to move off.

LONG-TROTTING

Long-trotting, especially during the summer months when the river is low and the water gin clear, calls for careful and thoughtful angling. The equipment consists of a rod of approximately 9 ft 6 ins, not too whippy, as a long line has to be lifted from the water. The reel should be very free-running. The monofilament line should be on the fine side, say 4 lb to 6 lb breaking strain.

The float should be on the big side to take a dozen shot, or better still, a barrel lead, as this does not bruise the cast and can be plugged at either end with a matchstick. A broad top float is best as it can be seen 50 yds away.

Your cast and hook must be a matter of choice, but there is no necessity to fish too fine. Do not put a shot on your hook length.

GROUNDBAIT

We now come to the most important item, that of groundbaiting the swim correctly. A good supply is necessary because of the fast stream, and great care should be taken in its preparation. All the water from well-soaked bread (stale) should be squeezed out and the bread kneaded into a soft paste.

In the summer the best swims are the natural ones, between weeds if possible, and for preference one which has a clean bottom.

Having decided on your swim, it must be groundbaited. If fishing from a punt, do not make the common mistake of either throwing your groundbait upstream or just in front of the punt. Both methods are wrong. Throw your groundbait, when you have decided on the line or course your float will take, at least 20 ft downstream from the punt, and if necessary weight it with a stone to stop it rolling along the bottom.

The reason for throwing it so far from the punt is because fish are curious, and will work upstream to the source of supply coming down, and you do not want them to come near the punt otherwise the flash of the rod and movement in the punt would frighten them away again. Collect your fish at a spot where they cannot observe you, for remember, the water is clear and perhaps shallow, and you strike at the end of every swim down.

It is advisable before groundbaiting to make sure you have a fairly long swim, so try it out after plumbing the depth and so save groundbait. Nothing is so upsetting as to find after groundbaiting that the swim is not suitable.

When baiting up, always show the barb of the hook. When fishing shallow water, the following procedure should be adopted: be careful not to trot down too far to commence with. Remember that fish are working up to the groundbait and you have to bring your float back to the punt again, and in doing so the passage of the float right over the swim, which may be anything up to 50 yds, would naturally disturb them. So fish the stream in sections for periods of from five to ten minutes (Figure 25).

Start off by trotting down 15 to 20 yds from the punt, to a point 'A' passing over the ground bait each time. Keep this up for the stipulated time, and then trot down from 'A' to a point 'B', say approximately 30 yds. And here again I must impress on you not to come back beyond point 'A', that is, 20 yds from the punt, and fish between these points again for a few minutes. If unsuccessful, trot down farther to a point 'C', and fish again for a few minutes between points 'B' and 'C'.

Continue like this until you have reached the end of the swim.

In this way each section has a complete rest from any disturbance, and it is surprising how by careful manipulation in the way described, good results are obtained even when fishing in 18 ins of water.

You now start the whole procedure over again. It is advisable, when bringing your float back to the punt, to point the rod to the bank. By so doing you keep the float out of the swim to a great extent. Do not wind in at express speed, when fishing shallow water. After groundbaiting, liberally at first, continue afterwards with small amounts. Little and often is the policy.

Long-trotting from the Bank

The procedure is much the same as when fishing from a punt. Throw the groundbait well downstream more especially when the water is clear and shallow. Persevere with breadcrust more often and use it continuously during the last hour.

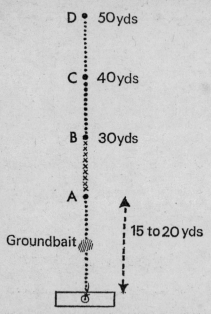

Figure 25 Fish from punt to A for five to ten minutes. Fish from A to B for five to ten minutes and so on. Do not bring float back beyond A when fishing A to B, or beyond B when fishing B to C. Strike at the end of every swim. Recover the float, when possible, out of the line of the swim

Long-trotting with Floating Maggots or Crust

A very thin piece of cork is glued or bound to the hook shank. Only enough is needed to give buoyancy to the hook and three or four maggots. This is not necessary if the bait is to be crust.

The equipment necessary for this style of fishing – rod, line and reel, is the same as for float fishing. The float should be on the big side – one, taking a dozen shot, or better still, a barrel lead. To the top of the float you now bind a small ring. On the bottom ring of the float attach 9 ins of gut or nylon, and on to this put your shot or barrel lead, sufficient to weight the float down to within 2 ins of the surface of the water.

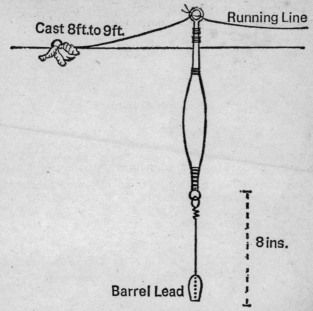

Figure 26 Long-trotting with floating maggots or crust

The reasons for using the big float and short, weighted length of gut, are:

(1) The float will peel off the line from the reel without assistance.

(2) It enables very shallow water to be fished.

(3) It eliminates wobble when you are reeling back.

The monofilament cast should be 9 ft in length. To the end of the cast attach the hook with cork body, bait with one or two maggots.

The position now is that everything is set up in much the same way as for float fishing but with this difference; your cast is tied to the top of the float, and likewise your running line. Make your cast if fishing from the bank, or drop into the water if fishing from a punt (Figure 26).

They go downstream, the maggots leading. Pay out line if the stream is sluggish, or let the stream do the work if you have a free-running reel as used for long-trotting. One can fish this way up to a distance of 30 yds, and although you may not see the maggots, it does not matter because your float gives you their whereabouts. Rises are readily seen and fish simple to hook because the fine floating line can be picked off the water in a split second.

Position on the river does not matter a great deal unless, of course, a wind is blowing. The water can be fast or sluggish, weedy or clear, for nothing seems to matter when fishing in this way.

Employing this system of fishing, swims can be fished which are impossible by ordinary methods. Those delightful runs under overhanging trees, close to the bank and between weed beds, etc, are made easy.

Floating crust can also be used in this way, the cork maggot then, of course, being unnecessary.

J. G. ROBERTS

Rudd

(See Figure 67, page 214)

The Rudd (*Scardinius erythrophthalmus*) is considered the most beautiful of all our freshwater fish. Big rudd are particularly striking. The rudd is not nearly so common as its near relative the roach but is fairly widely distributed throughout England, particularly in the Norfolk Broads which are noted for the magnificent specimens they produce each year. The rudd is rare in Scotland and Wales but abounds and grows to a great size in Ireland, where it is known as the roach by many of the local people.

IDENTIFICATION

The rudd has a deep body and its depth is usually more than one-third of the total length without the tail or caudal fin. It has a silvery body and large scales like roach, these scales being often tinged with gold, particularly in larger fish. The fish has a golden iris, with a red spot, and brilliant scarlet fins and the whole effect can be very beautiful. The colouring of rudd gets darker, richer and more brilliant with age. The back of the rudd is usually greenish-brown in colour. The rudd is sometimes confused and mistaken for the roach and ways of avoiding this and identifying the two species are described in the section on roach fishing.

SPAWNING

Rudd usually spawn towards the end of April into June when the water temperature has risen above 18°C (64°F). They spawn in similar places to roach, seeking the shallow sheltered bays. Rudd are not weakened by spawning to the same extent as roach, so are usually in good condition when the coarse fishing season opens on June 16th.

RATE OF GROWTH

Other things being equal rudd will grow more quickly than roach. In very good water the young fish should have reached ½ lb by the third year and 3 lb after about eight years. Rudd breed prolifically in still water if there are plenty of weedy shallows. Because of this small shallow ponds are usually overstocked with stunted specimens as there is not enough food for all of them. There are, however, notable exceptions to this so always give a small water a thorough trial, especially if it drains good land or if used extensively by cattle or horses.

SHOALS

Rudd swim about in shoals which may vary in size from a dozen or so to several hundreds. Unlike roach, shoals often consist of fish of varying sizes. The biggest rudd are commonly found in the centre or near the rear of the shoal.

HABITAT

Rudd are fish of quiet waters and are at home in shallow lakes, ponds, canals, slow-moving rivers or the quiet stretches of fast ones. They do not thrive in acid water.

LOCATING RUDD

Rudd, shallow water and weed go together, particularly early in the season when they will spend much of their time feeding in the vast weed beds which are a feature of rich shallow lakes. As the summer goes on they will be found in clearer water but seldom very far from weed beds. Rudd do not like wind so look for them in the shallow bays on the sheltered side of a lake. On very calm days, particularly if the weather is very warm and cloudy, conditions we seldom experience unfortunately, rudd will cruise up and down in the centre of the lake, near the surface.

In rivers, search the water of medium depth, again near weed beds and often close to the bank. If the water is very low and the weather hot they will sometimes be in the shallow streamy runs in or near the centre of the river and over weed beds if possible. As winter approaches rudd retire to the deeper quiet water where they will feed on mild days.

FEEDING HABITS

Unlike roach, rudd feed only occasionally on the bottom. They feed principally between mid-water and the surface and often take flies and other insects actually off the surface. They do not feed in winter as readily as roach, and only occasionally in still waters when the water temperature falls below 5°C (45°F). Rudd delight in warm calm days with low cloud cover. During these conditions they feed practically continuously throughout the long summer day. Rudd generally stop feeding if a cold wind develops and freshens. Main items of food are flies and their larvae, and larvae of insects, small snails which adhere to submerged vegetation and the underside of water-lily leaves, and vegetable matter.

ANGLING METHODS

These will be very similar to those described for roach. Remember, however, to fish near the surface. Start a few inches below the surface and gradually increase the depth down to mid-water. Rudd are greatly attracted by a bait which sinks slowly in the water, so dispense with weight if at all possible. If not, bunch the shot under the float and the bait will still sink slowly.

Groundbaiting will seldom be necessary when rudd fishing because of the fishes' surface feeding habits. Pieces of crust thrown on to the water and allowed to float sometimes attract rudd. Favourite baits are bread, in some form, maggots and worms. These should be fairly large, as in roach fishing, to avoid the small fish.

J. G. ROBERTS

Bream

(For identification, see Appendix I)

There are two British species of freshwater bream, namely the Common or Bronze Bream (*Abramis brama*) and the Silver or White Bream (*Blicca bjoerkna*). The latter is sometimes known as the breamflat.

The bronze bream is widely distributed throughout England and also occurs in Southern Scotland and in parts of Wales. It abounds in Ireland and is common practically everywhere in the limestone areas of that country. The silver bream is to be found chiefly in Norfolk and in the Fen country where it is plentiful. Distribution elsewhere is local.

IDENTIFICATION

There should be little difficulty in identifying bream. The body of a bream is deep and very compressed behind the ventral fin, the tail is deeply forked and head small when compared to the rest of the body. Young bronze bream are silvery in colour but this gradually changes to a yellowish brown and eventually to a dark bronze in large fish. The back is a dark grey or black and the belly white. Dorsal, tail and anal fins are dark grey, the pectoral and ventral light grey, darkening at the tips. The silver bream changes colour very little throughout its life and, unlike the bronze bream, retains the dominant silvery appearance. Young bronze bream are often mistaken for silver bream and *certain* identification is not possible without examining the teeth, which are in the throat. The pectoral and ventral fins of a silver bream are often a shade of red and differ in colour from those of bronze bream. Colour variations in fish however are wide and are an uncertain means of identification.

SPAWNING

Bream usually spawn about mid-May, sometimes into June depending on the weather conditions and water temperature. During this period the males have white tubercles on the scales which are rough to touch. If weather conditions are favourable bream may be observed spawning close inshore where they recover rather slowly from the spawning act and are seldom in good condition before August.

RATE OF GROWTH

Bream overstock small waters, rather like rudd, and seldom grow to a useful size unless they have plenty of room. In suitable water bronze bream should attain a weight of 10 lb in about twelve years and may eventually reach 15 lb. The English record bronze bream weighed 12 lb 14 oz and was taken from Great Cornard in July 1971. On most English waters a bream over 3 lb is regarded as quite a good fish, and one over 5 lb of specimen weight. Each year a number of bream are taken over 8 lb but these numbers are small when compared with the enormous amounts of bream which are caught. The silver bream is a much smaller fish than the bronze and specimens of between 1 lb and 2 lb are considered good fish.

SHOALS

Bream are distinctly a shoal fish and these will consist of fish which are, more or less, of even size. Shoals will vary in size from fifty or even less if the fish are large to several hundreds and sometimes thousands if the fish are very small. In a good water bream weighing about 3 lb will be in a shoal consisting of about 200 fish.

HABITAT

Bream thrive best in large deep lakes which have a mud bottom and are naturally a fish of quiet deep waters. Bream are common in most slow-moving rivers where they often attain a useful size. The majority of canals, in England, contain large stocks of bream in certain stretches. These fish are not usually up to the standard of those in rivers but there are some notable exceptions. Like most other fish, bream do not thrive in acid waters, however big or deep they may be.

LOCATING BREAM

In a lake there should be little difficulty in locating these fish as bream, when feeding, roam over a wide area in search of their food.

If you have groundbaited well in deep water bream will almost certainly find it and start feeding. Rivers are much different. There are certain stretches which hold bream and have done so for as long as anyone can remember, and others, perhaps just as likely looking, that do not. If you are fishing in one of the barren stretches groundbaiting is unlikely to attract them from their recognized haunts. River bream are usually to be found in a wide part of a river where there is a good depth of water. If the current is not too strong, they spend much of their time feeding in or near the centre of the river, especially during warm weather. Deep eddies below faster water are favourite spots for bream and deep swirling pools close to the bank are favourite haunts in winter, if the river is high. In hot sunny weather, during the afternoon, bream shoals usually come to the surface and lie in the sun for two hours or more. When they do this the backs and dorsal fins of the fish will show above the water from time to time and betray their presence.

FEEDING HABITS

Bream are bottom feeders, their diet consisting chiefly of the various forms of animal and vegetable life which are to be found in the mud at the bottom of a lake or river; when young these are principally small crustaceans and mosquito larvae, later, larger bottom-dwelling animals such as snails, small mussels, worms, as well as insect larvae. In warm and sunny weather, when the water temperature is high, bream feed a lot during the night and very early in the morning. This applies particularly to lakes and other still or perhaps semi-still waters such as canals. In *dull* warm weather bream feed at intervals throughout the day and night. In summer, early morning fishing is nearly always the most rewarding. Winter feeding is very spasmodic in lakes, when the water temperature falls below 7°C (45°F). In rivers good sport can often be obtained throughout the winter. As a prelude to serious feeding, bream are often to be seen rolling on the surface.

ANGLING METHODS

In rivers, as well as in still waters, ledgering either with or without a float is the best way to fish for bream. In a river, swimming the stream with the bait just dragging the bottom may sometimes bring better results but this is unusual.

If sizeable bream are expected tackle should be stronger than for roach or rudd. The line should be 4 lb to 6 lb breaking strain and hooks between sizes 4 and 10 to take large worms, bunches of smaller ones or maggots, and large pieces of bread flake, paste or crust all of which are first-class baits for bream. The tackle should be arranged so that the ledger weight is 2 ft from the hook. Large shoals of bream sometimes cruise and feed in the centre of a river and long casting may be desirable, but this is seldom necessary in a lake.

Heavy groundbaiting is essential on practically every water if one hopes to make good catches of bream. If it is possible to groundbait the same spot several days in advance of actual fishing the chances of a really big bag are greatly increased. Choose your spot with care and once you have decided on it stay there. Bream cover large areas in search of food and, if feeding, will eventually find your groundbait and start feeding on it. The larger the quantity of groundbait the longer the fish should stay with you. If it is not possible to groundbait in advance throw in 7 lb or more before starting to fish. When you have attracted the bream, and you know they are feeding, add more groundbait from time to time. Stale bread mixed with bran and made into stiff balls is as good a groundbait as any.

Weight for weight bream are inferior fighters to roach or rudd, they are a sluggish fish but because of their superior size and deep body, which offers considerable resistance to the water, sometimes need more skill in landing.

Barbel

(For identification, see Appendix I)

The Barbel (*Barbus Barbus*) is a hard-fighting fish which is not easily caught but its sporting qualities are well worth the special attention that has to be given to times, baits, methods and – above all – places, by anyone who wants to catch barbel other than by chance.

DISTRIBUTION

Widespread over the Central Plain of Europe, including northern France. East of the Danube a similar species is found in Asian rivers. Distribution in the British Isles is limited. From early years to the first quarter of this century it was (with odd exceptions) confined to the Thames and its tributaries; to the Hampshire Avon and the Dorset Stour; and to a group of rivers that flow to the North Sea across the Yorkshire Plain – Ouse, Nidd, Wharfe, etc.

These are still all good barbel rivers, but the introduction of new stock into other waters in recent years has increased its range considerably. Among these rivers are the Trent (once a famous barbel river in its own right and probably still holding some of the original stock); the Severn and some of its tributaries; and the Medway.

SIZE

Barbel weighing more than 20 lb are caught from time to time in Continental rivers, but in home waters a 10–pounder is a very satisfactory fish. Every season some 12- or 13-pounders are taken, yet a 14 lb 6 oz barbel caught in 1937 on the Hampshire Avon once shared the record with two others of the same weight taken in earlier years. The record in January 1972 was established at 13 lb 2 oz, following a reconsideration by the British Record (Rod caught) Fish Committee of all

barbel claims. The fact that a 16-lb barbel was caught out of
season by a salmon angler proves that record-breakers exist.

SPAWNING

Like most other fish barbel gather together to spawn. They
like smooth bottoms of fine gravel or coarse sand in relatively
shallow water, though this may be as deep as 10 ft, and when
they are so gathered they can be seen from suitable vantage
points by the score. Fish of all sizes from a pound upwards
can be seen milling about, and the would-be barbel catcher
might well say: 'This is the place to fish when the season
opens.' Unfortunately it never works out like that. It is clear
that barbel do not live where they spawn and long before mid-
June they will have dispersed to their chosen parts of the river.
In the weeks immediately following spawning they seem to
seek the fastest-running water they can find – at the base and
run-offs of weirs and in fast shallow glides in rivers.

FINDING BARBEL

After spawning many of the fish will have moved long distances up- or downriver and taken up summer stations.
Barbel *are* caught in sluggish water but the places to seek
them, even long after spawning, are the fast runs below banks,
the places in weir pools where hollows have been made by the
conflicting currents and immediately below ledges where food
gathers, and in the clear runs of water between intensive weed
beds in the main part of the rivers. Many weir pools are
famous barbel grounds, but I have caught most of mine miles
from weir pools, many in only 4 or 5 ft of water.

There are few visible signs of barbel in weir pools because
of depth and broken water. Any weir pool that holds barbel
will have a local reputation and you can fish with confidence.

Although barbel are bottom feeders they will come to the
surface and roll like bream, the big red tail being an indication
of species as the fish turns down. On occasions they will leap
from the water. These are easy pointers to the presence of
barbel in a swim.

In the open river barbel can sometimes be seen in their lies,
though it is necessary to look closely for some time until the
eyes are focused on the bottom. From above the fish are well

camouflaged, but as they move or turn a glint of silver from their sides may give them away. This is most likely to be seen in the swift runs between beds of weed streamed out by the current. When they are seen in these runs they are generally feeding and the places are obviously those into which to put a bait.

METHODS AND TACKLE

The two main methods for barbel are ledgering and long-trotting.

A 10 ft rod of the Avon Mk IV type is suitable for both. The reel can be the one with which you feel most comfortable. I generally use a 4½-inch centre-pin for long-trotting and a fixed-spool for ledgering. Lines can be from 6 to 9 lb breaking strain. Barbel are powerful fighters and if you know yourself to be rather hard-handed when playing a fish you can use the heavier strengths.

The ledger is accepted tackle for fishing the weir pools though those of suitable depth can be fished by long-trotting. The ledger angler who has made a study of the pool and knows the ledges and holes at the bottom will do better than the haphazard caster. Most pools have many snags and some have only small areas of clean bottom. A rolling ledger is an advantage where the bottom is known to be clear. Where snags are numerous a fixed ledger with the hook about 1 ft from the weight is a safer method. In the last case an Arlesey Bomb, or similar lead with an in-built swivel, may be better than the link ledger if the bait has to be held down to a very definite small area. In all other cases, whether rolling or static, the link ledger is, in my opinion, the ideal ledger weight for barbel fishing. It can almost instantaneously be adapted to anything from a slow flow to a strong current.

The ledger can also be a killing method in the open river, where the bait can be drifted or cast into known holes or into beds of weed. In the second case it is well to fish upstream into the weeds. The tackle can then be recovered, for rebaiting, with the flow of the weed instead of against it.

With a floating bait (crust, etc) the hook should be within 3 ins of the weight. With baits that sink naturally, 1 ft is more suitable. Some anglers (notably those on the Hampshire Avon) prefer trails up to 3 ft.

Long-trotting is no different in principle for barbel than for other fish. The float should be set about 1 ft higher than the depth of the water and the split shot (or a pierced bullet for strong currents) set at the exact depth. The bait will thus trip the bottom a few inches ahead of the weight.

FOOD AND BAITS

Barbel are almost exclusively bottom feeders, their underhung mouths making other feeding difficult. Their natural food consists mainly of worms, snails, mussels, insect larvae, fish eggs and any small fish they can catch, the last-named being normally bottom dwellers such as bullheads, gudgeon and loach. Much of their food is detected through the two pairs of feelers, called barbules or barbels, but this process obviously cannot work with a live fish. The way in which a barbel snatches a minnow bait shows that it does not rely entirely on touch and smell.

Lobworms were once regarded as the one, and almost only, bait for barbel. They are still excellent baits. Many barbel have been caught on maggots, usually by anglers fishing for other species, but the main baits used by modern barbel anglers are lobworms; minnows, alive or dead; especially for long-trotting; cheese; cheese paste; crust. In addition to these ordinary baits many barbel are now taken on chunks of raw sausage, beef or pork, and of tinned luncheon or similar meats. These baits are most likely to succeed in rivers where the fish have become used to them. It will be noted that all these baits are among those taken by chub, and since barbel and chub often share the same habitat it was probably chub anglers who discovered the usefulness of sausage and meat baits for barbel.

Small quantities of groundbait may induce the fish to start feeding, but it should not be overdone. A ball of soaked bread mixed with some of the hook bait is sufficient, but it must be made to settle where it is wanted, ie, a couple of yards upstream of the area which is being fished.

KENNETH MANSFIELD

Chub and Dace
(For descriptions, see Appendix I)

The Chub (*Leuciscus cephalus*) is a highly popular angler's fish for it answers most of the sportsman's requirements. It is widely distributed in England: it is found in large and small rivers and occasionally in still waters: it grows to a good size – 3 lb being very ordinary: it takes baits of all sorts fished by any standard method: and once hooked it puts up a fine sporting fight, especially in the first few moments when it seeks to reach its nearby retreat.

Like other coarse fish it spawns in the spring, congregating in fairly shallow water over clean river beds in order to do so.

HABITAT

This tends to differ with the seasons. Immediately after spawning the fish seek fast water, presumably for cleansing purposes, and there they feed voraciously and with little of the extreme caution which characterizes them at other times.

In summer and early autumn they tend to move into waters with a more gentle current, living in shoals which may comprise anything from half a dozen to two dozen fish. Favourite chub lies are in fairly deep water in a slow current beneath overhanging trees and bushes. This is where a watcher may study chub. Providing he be motionless and well hidden he can see them cruising around below the surface, taking anything that is brought to them, but ready to rise to any fly that alights on the surface, or to any of the multitude of caterpillars, grubs and other insects that drop from the overhanging foliage. There is no dashing take: sometimes one of the bigger fish of the shoal, normally keeping rank below the lesser fish, will see some attractive item and come up to shoulder aside the opposition to seize it. Then there may be a slight flurry, but all one normally sees is a fish rising as if in a lift, two open white and rubbery lips, the disappearance of the prey and slow sinking away. Chub are extremely shy, but when frightened there is no wild dash. They drop into the depths and there seek their sanctuary.

It is usually difficult to present a bait to fish in such places except by dapping, but there are many chub rivers that do not possess these overhung stretches, and here the feeding pattern must be different, as it is at times in the rivers so far described. In cold or inclement weather when there is no sun-warmed calm surface water to tempt them aloft – and in rivers where the peaceful situations do not exist at any time – the chub tend to feed deep, or, where there is no great depth, to move out into the main stream, feeding close to the bottom, preferably over sand or small gravel and especially in the narrow runs between clumps of weeds.

Wherever they feed, one thing is certain. Nearby is a safe place to which they can retreat when disturbed or resting. This can be a hole in the bank, a cavity among tree roots, a spot in a labyrinth of twisted snags or any other place where they feel themselves safe from predators – human or otherwise.

Chub continue to feed with appetite in water temperatures that put many other species off. Like many other species they prefer the deeper reaches and holes in cold weather, but although they can be caught in the depths there is evidence to show that they like to move into relatively shallow water – over a sunken shelf, for example – when they come on the feed.

METHODS

Chub can be caught by all the standard methods – float fishing, long-trotting and all types of ledgering. Ledgering is probably the best method for fishing the streams and weedy runs, with a running or light ledger. The angler can by this means keep well away from his quarry. Long-trotting produces the same advantage, but unless fishing from a punt the opportunities for long-trotting are few. Float fishing is a good method if the angler can remain hidden from the fish, and it is sometimes possible to float a bait down to them in their favourite tree-shaded haunts.

Chub have been caught on more varied baits than any other

British fish, but favourites are cheese, cheese paste, worms and crust. In rivers where they are educated to it they readily take lumps of sausage or tinned meat. They have big mouths, and a 2-lb chub can easily take a small whole crayfish, so baits (and hooks) should be on the large size.

DAPPING

Chub are the fish most often caught by dapping, the method now described. The chub must be observed feeding near the bank and close to the surface – in the conditions described above under trees and bushes. Tackle consists of a rod with a free-running line on which is threaded a pierced bullet, stopped a foot or so above the hook. The hook is baited with a grub, caterpillar, worm or other natural bait, or a large bushy artificial fly.

The angler, having found his chub, creeps up behind cover and pokes his rod over the top of the bushes. He then lets the line down slowly, until the bait reaches the water. It should appear to be a natural gift from heaven, and if it does, a take will be almost instantaneous. You may be in a position to see the fish take. If so, do not strike by sight. Wait until you feel the pluck as the fish turns down.

If the foliage prevents your putting the rod over the top of it, you may be able to achieve the same result by poking the rod through some gap. If this has to be so you must wind sufficient line around the rod tip to reach the water. When the tip is clear of the bushes the rod is turned so that the line unwinds and gradually reaches the water.

GROUNDBAITING

Groundbait is useful for both chub and dace when float fishing, ledgering or long-trotting. Small balls of soaked bread mixed with specimens of the hook bait are cast down-stream. Chub and dace are likely to follow the small particles of food upstream until they reach the source, which is where your bait will be.

Dace

Dace (*Leuciscus leuciscus*) are elegant little fish which can provide considerable sport if one is content with fish that will normally weigh only ounces. A 1-lb dace is a good specimen.

They like streams and rivers with a fairly swift current, and in these they feed mainly close to the bottom, but rise for surface feeding in warm weather when there is a hatch of fly on the water.

They are often found in company with chub, in large schools, and, like chub, they are omnivorous feeders. Their mouths are much smaller and small baits are desirable. Groundbait as for chub.

They can be caught by light float fishing or ledger fishing, but the tackle must be really light, for the 'take' is so swift that an instantaneous strike is necessary. They have an uncanny way of stripping a hook even of a worm before the strike gets home. On one occasion on the Kennet I lost bait after bait while light ledgering for dace, and caught my first fish only when I struck as soon as I thought my weight was down and before I felt a pluck.

FLY FISHING

Dace readily take artificial flies when the sun tempts them to the surface. Other coarse fish that take flies are rudd (the readiest takers), chub and roach.

For fly fishing you must have a fly rod and fly line. Equipped with these and some slight casting ability you can have a lot of fun on summer evenings with these four species – dace, rudd, chub and roach. They are not fussy about fly patterns, but if you are deliberately after chub something big and bushy is perhaps the best.

Carp

(For identification, see Appendix I)

DESCRIPTION

The carp in its native state is the Common Carp (*Cyprinus carpio*). Two distinct varieties have been bred from it, namely, the leather carp and the mirror carp (for descriptions, see Appendix I). The varieties, and crosses between them, are nowadays usually referred to collectively as king carp.

On the Continent, where they hold freshwater fish in very high esteem for culinary purposes, the carp is probably the most sought-after fish for the table, and it was for this reason that the varieties referred to were bred – by selective breeding. They grow very much quicker and very much larger than the original common variety, and therefore the breeders are able to sell them at an earlier age, and not wait so long before reaping their harvest.

Unfortunately for the angler, as regards record fish, the varieties all freely inter-breed, and consequently there are fish that are not of any of the three distinct varieties. After a few generations of inter-breeding, the progeny often revert back to the appearance of their forefathers, namely the common carp, and although biologically they are identical with common carp, they have however inherited the growth rate, and the large size, of the king carp.

For this reason the accepted records for carp are inclusive of all varieties, there being no separate record for leather or mirror carp, owing to the difficulty of differentiating between the various inter-breeds. There is one other species of carp – the smaller crucian carp (see Appendix I for description).

The carp is not indigenous to this country and the first known reference to it was in 1496. It is believed to have been introduced into England from the Continent for the stew ponds of the monasteries.

It is from this stock that we now get our 'naturalized' strain of carp, which are known as 'wild' carp. They are much more slender than the common carp, and do not grow so large. A 12-pounder would be an exceptionally good one. When hooked, the speed of these 'wild' carp is amazing, and although they seem to 'burn' themselves out quicker, the fight is often a long one. The heavier carp pull much harder, and use their weight to great advantage, and although some of their runs are fast, they usually fight harder but slower than the 'wild' carp.

FEEDING

The food of carp is of a nature that seems to belie their great size, as it is mostly of very minute variety. Organisms such as bloodworms, algae, various forms of larvae, snails, water fleas (daphnia), shrimps and other insects are eaten. Vegetable matter, silk weed and young plants, all form part of their varied diet.

In early morning and late evening, if one is careful enough to approach the fish without being observed, it is possible to watch them feeding on the shallows, often stirring up clouds of mud as they dig down for food. I rather fancy that they can suck up fine mud and filter it through their gill rakers, thus retaining the food within. The rushes at the edges of pools and lakes, and where they grow in the shallow parts, can be seen being literally thrust aside as if by some unseen hand, as a large fish forces his way through them in search of food. When carp are observed feeding in this way, except sometimes in the vicinity of groundbait, they can rarely be induced to take the angler's bait. However, they are well worth stalking at such times, as I *have* taken fish by laying my bait in the path presumed to be that which the fish would travel, and at least the angler has the advantage of knowing exactly where a fish is.

BUBBLERS

Sometimes, a feeding carp will betray his presence by causing a patch of very small bubbles, or a trail of small bubbles to appear on the surface of the water. Whether or not the carp discharges a certain amount of air from its air bladder to cause these bubbles, or whether or not they are caused by disturbing the gases from the mud at the bottom, I hesitate to say. I sometimes think that the fish for some reason is responsible, as if they were just disturbances of the bottom, the bubbles would be of varied size and appear in batches, whereas they are all very small and often continuous. I must admit that I have only on very few occasions witnessed these small bubbles, although the masses of bubbles caused by rooting on the bottom are often seen. Their keen sense of smell and their barbels no doubt help them tremendously when rooting in the mud.

SURFACE FEEDERS

When the carp cause waves to come from patches of water-lilies and other floating leaved plants, as they feed on the surface, they sometimes take a floating crust. They are, I fancy, feeding on snails and the jelly-like substance full of embryo snails.

Although most of their food is of a nature that would make it impractical to use as bait, they can be educated to take the angler's bait (see section on groundbait).

FEEDING TEMPERATURE

Carp rarely feed if the water temperature is below 13°C (56°F), and rarely if over 20°C (68°F). About 17°C (62°F) seems to be about the best feeding temperature. Sometimes, towards the end of the carp season, in September and October, they will feed well with the temperatures perhaps a little lower than those stated.

They are very much creatures of habit, and if you can find the 'run' of a carp, you can ambush him. Some follow a certain feeding path, and after observing this route, you can lay a bait on this path and await results.

BEST TIMES

The best times to fish for carp are late evening and early morning. If night fishing is allowed, the hours of darkness will also produce fish. The first hour or two after dusk is often very good, then for some reason they seem to stop feeding until an hour or two before the advent of daybreak. Although water temperature does control their feeding appreciably, the water before dawn must be colder than during the night, and although, as the sun rises, the shallows soon warm up – and they are the places to fish when this happens – it does not explain their activity prior to the rise in temperature. The fish sometimes feed through the day at the end of September and during October, but generally speaking, he who wishes to catch carp must be prepared to fish during the above times. Carp fishing is not for those who like their beds, it is a sport for others than the lazy.

HIBERNATION

The first frost brings to an end the carp season proper, as during the cold months the carp goes into a state of hibernation. The remarkable thing about this 'sleep' is that the fish are absolutely oblivious to anything around them. I heard of a pond that was drained during the winter, when live carp and tench were picked out of the mud and decayed vegetation on the bottom, without a movement.

This torpid condition does not seem to apply so much to rivers, as a friend and I, fishing the Thames at Twickenham for dace live bait, were greatly surprised when his gentles were taken by a carp of about 8 oz. It was a day when the sun did not appear and a white frost stayed with us all day. Periodically ice had to be sucked from the rod rings, but that did not deter this little fish from showing he was fighting fit.

Probably, the odd days in late September and October, when carp seem to lose all caution and feed ravenously, is a pre-hibernation 'stoking of the fire'.

TRANSPORTATION

A feature that should make the carp a favourite of angling clubs, is its easy transportability. They are able to live for many hours wrapped in a wet cloth, or in wet moss, and it is therefore obvious how this remarkable fact simplifies stocking projects.

WHERE TO FIND CARP

Distribution

Although not generally known, the carp is found as far north as the Fintry district of Scotland, but is more evenly distributed in the Midlands and Southern regions of England.

Wales contains carp waters, and recently they have been introduced into a private water in Co Westmeath, Ireland.

They are certainly well worth fishing for as far north as Yorkshire in suitable waters, and probably a little farther north than that county.

Type of Water
The sluggish habits of carp denote that they are mostly suited to still waters, and it is in these waters that the angler would best ply his skill if he is to be successful in his pursuit of carp.

They are found in lakes, ponds, reservoirs and various kinds of pits, ie, gravel pits, clay pits and the like. Canals also hold carp, and a few rivers have them in certain stretches, but rivers are not really worth fishing for them.

Small Waters
One very useful quality of the carp is that he will grow very large in a very small water, and it is a mistake to presume that if a pond is small it will not hold carp (if it holds any) of a size worth fishing for. I have taken quite a few carp of double figures in a pool which is much less than an acre, and where it is very hard to find more than 3 ft of water. This particular water also holds *small* tench, *small* roach, *small* bream and *small* crucian carp. If these had been removed I have no doubt that the carp would have grown very much larger.

Other Still Waters
The larger ponds and lakes which hold carp present more of a problem than the small water, as the whereabouts of the fish will be to some extent governed by the temperature, depth and wind direction. They are normally found in the close proximity of weeds, and this fact should be taken into consideration by the angler when trying to decide upon a swim. They do not like leaving the safety of this green jungle, and consequently are rarely found in open water.

Influence of Temperature
On very hot days the water will be too warm for the carp to feed, and they may be seen on the surface basking, hardly moving a fin. In water that is comparatively shallow, ie, no holes over 4 to 5 ft deep, as the sun goes down and the water cools, they will probably commence feeding in the shallowest

part of the lake, gradually moving to the deeper water as the temperature drops. Their feeding period may be short, as in these shallow waters, unless it is an exceptionally warm night, the whole of the water soon becomes too cold for them to feed, as there is no deep water to retain the heat. The clearer the night, the colder, and the quicker the temperature of the water will decrease. Where there are deep holes, ie, over 8 or 9 ft, the carp will retire to them as the water temperature drops, and will probably feed spasmodically during the night. These holes are also productive during the daytime later in the year.

It is difficult to state exactly how temperature affects carp, for, as with other fish, there are always exceptions. Sometimes an ideal day will produce not a run (possibly they have eaten their fill before one started fishing) whereas a bad day may well be productive. Experience has taught me to fish whenever possible, whether the day – or night – was good or bad for fishing.

Effect of Wind
On hot days, when the water temperature is above the feeding temperature of carp, a breeze springing up may well cause the

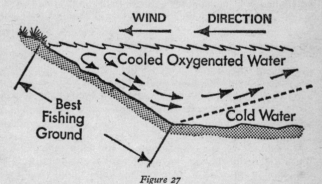

Figure 27

fish to feed. It may cool the water sufficiently, and it will move the surface water to the end towards which it is blowing. This will build up (Figure 27) and when this happens it is as well to fish *in the face of the wind*. This applies to most fish during the summer months.

Do not imagine by these observations that I mean carp

roam about all over the lake, as the wind and temperature drives them, but in larger waters it is possible that the carp at one end of the lake may be induced to feed, whereas those at the other end may not.

Observation

Finding feeding carp by observation, ie, looking for mud stirrers, and bubblers, has been mentioned earlier.

Canals and Rivers

To find carp in canals is not easy, and local knowledge is very necessary. The weedy stretches will of course be the places to try, but frequently in canals, one is confronted with miles of water all similar, and one is hard put to decide where to start. Well-worn pads on the bankside, made by anglers constantly fishing the same swim, may be worth a try, as although the anglers responsible may not have been fishing for carp, if groundbaiting has been consistent carp may be in the vicinity.

With rivers, the quieter reaches, backwaters and eddies, will be the places to fish, but unless a particular spot is known to hold a fair head of carp, they are so sparse and unevenly distributed in rivers as to be hardly worth the effort involved in trying to catch one.

SPAWNING AND GROWTH

(Note: I acknowledge with thanks the help given to me in the compilation of this section by Mr D. F. Leney, of the Surrey Trout Farm, Springhead, Shottermill, Haslemere, who breeds carp and has made an intensive study of them – D.L.S.)

Spawning

Unfortunately for the carp fisherman, the temperature of the British Isles during the spawning time of carp is sometimes too low for breeding to take place. Even though spawning takes place in suitable waters every year, a sudden drop in temperature will cause the death of all the eggs and carp fry. There is very little fear in this country of carp becoming a menace to our other fish population, as I believe has happened in certain parts of the United States and South Africa, where the prodigality of the carp has deteriorated fishing for other species. We could, in fact, do with more stocking projects involving the introduction of carp to suitable waters, as a replacement to the stunted roach and perch population that inhabits some of them.

The months of May and June are usually spawning months for carp, but with bad weather, spawning often extends into July. The carp, which normally lead a solitary existence, tend to congregate over their selected breeding beds, where the female is courted by several males. The female is sometimes distinguishable by being more swollen where the eggs are carried, and much softer in the belly than the males. In females which have spawned previously, the vent protrudes a little during the spawning period.

The eggs are shed singly, and the disturbance of the water, caused by the excitement of the fish, washes the eggs onto water plants, stones, twigs and the like, to which they adhere. The eggs, which are 1.5 mm in size, hatch in approximately 5 to 10 days depending on the water temperature, the resultant fry being about 5 mm long. Within 8 days or so, the yolk sac is absorbed and the tiny little fish start feeding on microscopic underwater life. Carp carry a tremendous number of eggs, which is nature's necessity to their survival. Mr D. F. Leney mentions an 8¼ lb fish which died at spawning time carrying 1¼ lb of eggs, and an 18 lb carp that held 860,000 eggs.

Growth and Age

At the present time there is a popular belief that waters which hold carp probably hold some very heavy fish, many pounds heavier than any that have been taken from them, and while it is possible that some waters, which are not properly fished for carp, do have fish in them a great deal heavier than those caught, I do not believe that there are many waters in the British Isles that hold 30– to 40–pounders. In the majority of carp waters a 10 lb fish is a good one, and a 20-pounder is an exceptionally large specimen. The common 'wild' carp rarely exceeds 12 lb in weight, and after trying to trace common carp above that weight, and having seen cases of 'common carp' above that weight, I have come to the conclusion that they are really king carp with common carp scaling.

The weight to which king carp will grow in exceptional waters has been amply proved by Mr Richard Walker, with his 44-lb carp (common carp scaling), and as the fish was a mere fourteen or fifteen years old the growth rate of this fish was amazing. These Redmire fish would probably grow to a weight of 50 or 60 lb when they were nearer the end of their life cycle, but I do not think there are other *known* waters in the country which would produce such fish. There probably *are* such waters, if the carp were introduced.

I would say here that anglers generally are much indebted to Mr Walker for his original and careful study of the carp as well as other coarse fish. Those not already familiar with his books are particularly referred to his *Still-Water Angling* and *Drop Me a Line*.

The following scale of the growth of king carp in this country is the average growth in suitable-to-good waters, and I am greatly indebted to Mr D. F. Leney for these approximate figures.

First year – 3 to 6 ins
Second year – 3 to 12 oz
Third year – 8 oz to 2 lb
Fourth year – 1½ to 4 lb

The fish probably start to spawn at four or five years old, and the growth rate will remain fairly constant afterwards. Thus, in an average water, a ten-year-old fish would go about 8 lb or so, but in a good water the same fish would weigh about 16 lb. On the Continent, they get a much faster growth than we do, as the water warms up quicker and remains at a much more constant temperature than in this country. Towards the end of their life, the growth of carp slows up, and they may lose weight eventually through loss of girth, although the length may increase slightly. Twenty-five years would be a fair age for carp to attain, but they have been recorded to live up to forty-seven years in captivity.

GROUNDBAITS

(Note: The author then discusses baits for carp, including paste, crust, balanced crust, worms and potatoes. These have all been described in the section on coarse fishing baits, but some special suggestions for ground baits for carp follow. Ed.)

One important factor towards success on some carp waters, is groundbaiting. I think the main point to be considered in groundbaiting for carp, is to *feed* them enough of the type of bait you are using, to *educate* them to eat it without fear. For this reason I always groundbait with the same size bait as I am fishing with. If I am fishing with large pieces of paste, I groundbait with large pieces of paste, if I am fishing with a potato, I groundbait with potatoes. In waters where there are other fish, it will be seen why the carp may take a potato in preference to bread, providing one has groundbaited with potato. The carp may hardly have had a chance to sample bread, whereas consistent groundbaiting with potato would have shown its value as food. Groundbaiting with worms also helps one's chances, if worms are to be the hook bait, but here again other fish may prove a nuisance.

In well-fished water containing other fish, if bread is to be used as bait, it sometimes is *not* desirable to groundbait at all. The other anglers should have thrown in sufficient bread to teach the carp to eat it, so they have already been educated to it. Groundbaiting by the carp angler will only more quickly lead smaller fish to his hook bait, so he is better off to wait for the solitary carp to find it first. In these waters, floating crust may be used to advantage, as the fish should be used to taking the bits of crust that drift into the edges, from other anglers groundbaiting. A few large crusts – so as not to be whittled down by the small stuff – should be thrown in, and attention paid to the direction of drift. It is no use throwing crusts in your swim if they float off to the other side of the lake. The best advice then is find a swim the other side of the lake. Any other surface food will be blown there as well, so always fish towards drift or wind, if fishing on the surface in the edge. In well-fished waters, the best fishing of this kind commences after the other chaps have gone home.

METHOD: PRELIMINARY TACTICS

For the angler who is able to fish for carp locally, his is a happy lot. If he is prepared to work for his fish – to prepare swims, groundbait prior to his fishing, regularly visiting the water solely for these and other non-angling purposes, then he is assured of much greater success.

Before the angler commences these preparations he must choose a swim, or preferably, two or three swims. There are many factors to be taken into consideration before choosing. One will see many anglers fishing in spots in which, if they hooked a large fish, they would find it almost an impossibility to land it.

The snags in the vicinity of the whereabouts of the fish, the weeds, and what types of weeds they are, the bankside, whether there are any marginal rushes where the angler hopes to land a fish should he hook one – all these factors and many more *must* be taken into account when choosing a swim.

Perhaps I can give an example of where choosing the position from which to fish will help ensure the landing of such fish. This particular example actually concerns carp fishing (in my club's water) and it will, I hope, illustrate my point.

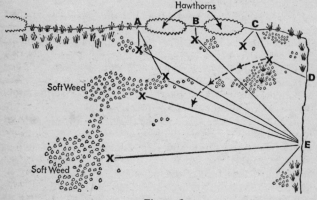

Figure 28

If one takes Figure 28 as a fair example of one of the corners of the pond, it will be seen that the marginal reeds – which extend from the bank for about 18 ft – and the hawthorn bushes, occupy nearly the whole length of the north bank. The only places that it is possible to fish from this bank in this particular corner, are marked A, B and C. They are very popular swims and the carp do feed in them, but most of the members just fish there for anything that comes along. Occasionally, very occasionally – one of them does hook a carp, and I have heard proudly told tales of 'how I was smashed up'. Why it is that the majority of fishermen simply fish a swim without taking into account the surrounds of the swim, I have no idea. But there is no doubt that they do. If they just looked around them they would see that in swim A, to their right, are masses of thickly groping reeds, in which a good fish will almost certainly tangle the line sufficiently to cause a break; to their left are hawthorns and brambles trailing into the water. Swim B has hawthorns and brambles on each side of it, and even the last rush of a large carp is often powerful enough to enable it to reach such sanctuaries as these, when they are not far away.

Swim C is not too bad, providing the angler fishing it moves round to his left, where he can apply sidestrain to keep the fish out of the hawthorns on his right, should it wish to run into them. Apart from the fact that an angler may let the fish swim out, and play it well out, he must play it *towards the danger area* to be landed.

Fishing from the swim marked D, my wife landed a carp of just on 10 lb. This fish ran in the direction of the dotted line, but was played to swim E by the line being lifted clear of the few reeds shown in the middle of the soft weed bed. If the fish had made for the nearest hawthorns, she could have applied considerable sidestrain by moving to her left. The only fish I have lost in this corner was lost through it going round those reeds. I intend to remove them one season.

However, the best position to fish the swims shown is from E, and apart from the fish mentioned, I have not lost any other from this position. The weed beds marked soft are such that a fish can easily be brought through them, and a fish running into them always stops, and thus helps one to play it. An interesting point is that in between these soft weed beds there is sparse weed, and along this the carp seem to rove in between the weed beds. A bait dropped on this track often produces a run, and I recently took a 15-pounder by a long cast to the farthest point of this track. Unlike the other swims, one is playing the fish *away from the danger area.*

Other waters present different problems, but the point I hope I have explained is, that it is no use hooking a carp if you cannot land the fish, but it is usually possible to work out some way to land it even if – as in this case – it means casting a long way.

Where there are reeds and rushes at the bankside extending for any distance from the shore, a clear patch must be made among them for the landing of fish. I do not mean where the angler is going to fish, as he may be removing the natural cover that these reeds and rushes provide, but somewhere in the immediate vicinity, to where he may play his fish, to be netted. A scythe is a very useful tool for this purpose, and if one can extend the handle, it will double its worth. The reeds should be cut right down to the roots, for it is the roots that the carp seems to get the line wrapped round. Once this has happened, it is 'au-revoir' to Mr Carp.

Water-lilies may be removed if they prove a nuisance, for they are the worst kind of plant for tackle smashing. Most other weeds and plants can be cleared simply by dragging them out. For this purpose I use two rake heads bound together and attached to a length of rope.

Groundbaiting should be commenced approximately a fortnight before the opening date, or whenever it is possible to pay a visit to the water. The bait to be used should be thrown in in fair quantities, enough to teach the carp to eat it, and to congregate in the chosen swims. Once they have become accustomed to the bait, groundbaiting once or twice a week should be sufficient to keep them interested. In a water that I have baited over a period, because I groundbait with the same size pieces as my hook bait, I prefer not to groundbait during my actual fishing time, and usually do so after I have packed up, to keep the fish interested till my next visit.

The carp fisherman who is arriving at a new water for the first time, should have a good look round the water, and use his water-craft to try to decide the whereabouts of the fish. When he has found a likely looking spot and groundbaited (bread is probably best on a new water, until one knows that the carp have other ideas) he should decide what method would best suit. Probably until proved otherwise he would be as well to start by ledgering, which is the best all-round method for results. One should always try to fish at the right time, during the last and first hours of daylight, and during the night. For those who have to travel a long way to their fishing, it is wise to arrive the previous evening and arrange to stop the night by the water, or at the nearest lodging-place.

LEDGERING FOR CARP

The most practical method of ledgering for carp is the most simple. The tackle required is merely a hook whipped or tied on to the end of the running line to which the bait is attached. This is then cast out to the desired spot and the angler awaits results. No lead, no split shot, no float, just bait is used to cast out the line. If I am using a potato for bait, I usually use eyed hooks, as this simplifies baiting. The line is threaded through the eye of a needle, and the needle and line passed through the potato from centre, to slightly *off-centre*. This ensures the potato will be evenly distributed on the hook, thus increasing the chances that they do not part company if making a long cast. The hook is then tied on and drawn back into the potato. Do not draw the hook right into the potato, the force of casting, if any distance, will do that – unless the potato is too hard – and for this reason, when peeling the potato after I have threaded the line through it, I leave a little of the peel, where the bend of the hook will be, to prevent the hook pulling right through with the force of the cast.

If whipped hooks are preferred, the use of a proper baiting needle to thread the looped end of the hook-line through the potato is necessary. The whole lot is then passed through a loop at the end of the line, and one is ready to cast out. I like to dye the hook length a dark brown. To do this, I soak the nylon in a 4 per cent solution of silver nitrate for half an hour, then hang it in the sunlight. The depth of brown required can be arrived at by the amount of time the nylon is left in the sunlight. Afterwards I wash the nylon in warm water.

With the fixed-spool reel, casting is a simple matter as long as one does not cast too far. If one has put a little too much force in the cast, and it is overshooting its mark, the first finger of the casting hand should be dropped gently onto the spool. If done correctly, the line will flip out between the finger and the spool, and with a little practice it is soon possible to slow up and stop the bait at the desired spot. I always overcast and drop the bait where I want it by this method, as it is much easier than trying to judge the exact force required to project an object to a certain point.

If a centre-pin reel, or a multiplying reel, is used for carp fishing, the line must first be paid out onto a piece of mackintosh, cloth or something else on which to coil the line prior to the cast, so that it will not catch in snags. If one coils the line from the reel to the mackintosh, and then reverses the order of the coils, it will be found that during the cast the coils come from the top of the pile, and save any fear of tangling. When the correct distance has been cast, it is best to tie a couple of turns of cotton tightly to the line close to the reel. The correct amount of line can then be drawn off each time a cast is made, to enable the angler to cast the same distance again. The ends of the cotton should be nipped off very close, so that there is no hindrance whatsoever of the line passing through the rod rings as a carp takes the bait.

When a carp does take the bait, the fish generally bolts just about as fast as it can go, and the line tears out. The effect of this on a tight line would be that the fish would at least eject the bait. If the fish hooked itself, it would mean either a broken line or rod, if the rod didn't decide to take a dive into the lake. To counteract this tendency on the carp's part to remove itself to another district at all possible speed, with a fixed spool reel, the pick-up arm is left in the open position. The line is then free to run through the rings until the angler decides to strike. With other reels, the line must be drawn off the reel, coiled and reversed on the mackintosh sheet, the same as if one was about to cast out.

After having made one's cast, the rod should be placed in a rod rest to await the arrival of a fish. This rod rest must be such that the line can run freely through it as through the rod rings, for there must be no possible hitch to cause a carp to drop the bait. I have before me at the moment a rod rest which aptly fulfils these requirements, and which is more or less a copy of the rests designed by the Carp Catchers' Club (Figure 29). The twisted wire top screws into the upright stick. The screw-in part is an asset, as I use this for the attachment of my electric bait alarm. As the thread is standard, it leaves the metal rod part, useful for other purposes, ie, a short gaff or landing net handle for use when spinning. They are now available in most fishing tackle shops.

Usually at the commencement of fishing, the line – especially a fine nylon monofilament (6 to 8 lb) – is exceedingly buoyant, and the resultant drag through the floating line can be very annoying. I find that this can be overcome by putting the tip of the rod under the water, and gently pulling the line until it is all sunk. If there is a wind, and the water is at all rough, the little waves breaking over the line will soon sink it.

To save the wind blowing out the line between the rod top and the water, the rod top should be fished as near the water as possible. Sometimes a strong wind will catch the line between the rod rings, and to save this annoyance, the lightest piece of twig (but heavy enough to counteract the trouble) that can be found, is placed over the line. I also use this twig as a bite indicator, and place it across the line, slightly to the rear of the fixed spool reel as in Figure 29. As it is to the rear of the reel, it serves the double purpose of stopping the line being blown off the spool by a wind behind one, and stopping the nylon monofilament from springing off the spool of its own accord, which it is sometimes apt to do. When a bite

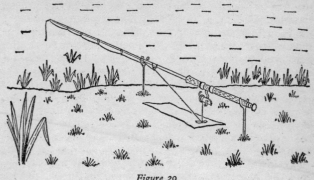

Figure 29

takes place, the stick is moved to one side – sometimes it is *shot* out of the way – owing to the action of the running fish tightening the line. Another rod rest, of any type, at the rear end of the rod, helps keep the tackle clear of the ground, and enables one to fish the rod pointing towards the water if so desired.

When an exceptionally long cast is to be made, ie, over 40 or 50 yards, a lead then becomes a necessary evil to enable this distance to be attained. I prefer to use a lead with a built-in swivel of the Arlesey bomb type, which reduces resistance to a minimum.

A small split shot is placed about 3 ft above the hook, and the lead is free to run above the shot. A lead is useful to enable one to fish with a crust, which would otherwise float. In this case the shot is nipped on the line only 2 or 3 ins above the hook, and the crust floats above the lead. This method has two advantages in that it hides the lead by having the crust suspended over it, and also the fish cannot feel the line, which is directly below the crust.

If one is fishing a swim near the same bank on which one is seated, it is advisable to move a little way from the actual swim, and cast parallel with the bank up to it. This will ensure that sufficient line is sunk between the rod and the bait, so as not to alarm the fish. Another point in its favour is that the angler is not fishing directly over his swim, and in most cases the farther away from the fish the angler is, the better the results usually are. (The exception is when fishing floating crust directly beneath the rod top.)

If fishing near the bank, the angler must take extra care not to disturb the fish by excessive movement and stamping of feet, etc. Sober clothes are also a must when fishing clear waters. White shirts and light summer clothes can be seen for miles, and so can the angler who stations himself with his magnificent physique silhouetted against the skyline. The carp will not be impressed. When one is quiet, and treats the fish with respect, it is amazing the amount of knowledge that can be acquired by watching them. Carp like the shallows, and in clear water this fondness of grubbing over such shallow areas of the bottom, enables the angler to view them a great deal.

When ledgering with lobworm, if a longish cast is to be made, I find that it is safer to hook the worm through twice to save the tendency to throw it off the hook. For short casts, hooked through once is sufficient. To hook on the lobworm twice, I insert the hook completely through the worm, about a third of the way down from the head, and re-insert it about two-thirds of the way down. This leaves the hook nearer the tail than the head. As for some reason nearly all fish seem to take a worm tail first, I find this an asset. I prefer to strike sooner when using worms, as I am sure that the fish can feel the hard metal of the hook, and are more likely to eject it than paste or potato. I strike fairly soon with a run on crust too, for the same reason, and because crust will come off the hook very easily.

If groundbaiting is carried out, it should be thrown out to the spot where the bait is to be lying, by means of checking with a mark. If the bait is always cast in the direction of the same mark, it should be somewhere on the path created by the groundbait.

FISHING FOR CARP WITH A FLOAT

This is a form of fishing which for carp I do not like a great deal. I prefer to have nothing on the line at all that can cause even the minimum of resistance. If one uses a float, one has to use lead, even if only to make sure the line adjacent to the hook is well and truly laying along the bottom. I have only once found a float useful to me in carp fishing, and probably given a little more thought to the case in question I could have done without it then. A certain gravel-pit that I used to fish for carp has a gradually shelving bed, which is absolutely covered in the edges with old tins, bottles, pram wheels and every other conceivable kind of rubbish, that accumulates in the edges of gravel-pits with adjacent housing estates.

This shelving bed extends for about 40 ft to a depth of some 4 ft and then drops down sharply to a depth of 12 ft. The carp mostly seemed to feed in this 12 ft of water, and as this is one of the shallower parts of the pit, most of the other swims being 14 ft and over, this is understandable.

If one tried fishing this swim in the normal ledgering manner – just casting out the bait and letting the line sink, the line would catch in one or other of the many obstructions in the edge. If one put on a running lead, so as to keep the line tight between lead and rod top, with the rod top high enough to have the line clear of the rubbish, the line came into contact with the ledge where the bed dropped away sharper. The only answer was to use a float.

The float tackle I used in this instance will suit admirably for most other forms of carp fishing where a float is necessary, or if the angler prefers it. I used a porcupine quill which would carry two small shot, one of which I nipped on about 3 ft from the hook, and the second one about 4 ft from the hook. The depth was so adjusted that there was 15 ft of cast between the hook and float, consequently the bottom shot and 3 ft of cast were lying on the bottom. The other shot was carried by the float, clear of the bottom, so that it would not be carried by a fish, should one take the bait. In fact it would help overcome some of the buoyancy of the float and thus slightly reduce drag.

After baiting with a generous helping of paste (the best bait to use at this pit for carp) I used to cast beyond the spot that I required to fish, and then gently draw back the float until it was half cocked. This made sure that the 3 ft between hook and shot was straight, and there was not any fear of the line being suspended above the bait. The float being half cocked, ensured that the bottom shot was resting on the bed with the 3 ft of cast. One may think I am fussy about this 3 ft between hook and shot, but I think it very important that when a carp picks up the bait he should not come into contact with any line.

If one imagines he may be well over 2 ft in length, unless a fair margin is left he can easily touch the line. Probably 4 ft between hook and shot would be better. I used to attach the float by the bottom ring only, as this helped to sink the line between it and the rod top, eliminating any surface drag. The fixed spool reel was left with an open pick-up, so that the fish could run off line as with a normal ledger. A stick was placed over the line which was drawn sufficiently tight to lie over the rubbish.

In the deeper water, the carp never took a bait so fast as in the shallow water, and when hooked, if allowed to keep well down, they would bore more, and not make the long runs expected of carp in shallow water. I never lost a carp there through the rubbish, but as they mostly ran between 4 and 8½ lb – the largest I caught there – I would not like to say if I would have landed a large one. I did hook one largish carp there, but after playing it for about ten minutes the hook pulled out. The one glance I had suggested that the fish may have gone to 15 lb. Unfortunately I no longer have permission to fish this water.

I found the same method suitable after dark, and by over casting and drawing the tackle in until the mark on my line was reached, I knew I was in the right spot. The line was watched for a bite instead of the float. The only other way of getting at the swim, owing to the pit being surrounded by bushes and trees, would have meant a cast of about 80 yds.

The above method is a well-known method of taking coarse fish and is known as 'shot-ledgering'. I have described it in detail here to show how this method can be applied to over-come difficulties, which although it was successful with the use of a float, the float would *not* have been used if it could have been avoided.

If one uses this method for fishing a swim reasonably near, and requires a floating line, the float is not attached solely by the bottom ring, it may cause the line to sink. The line is threaded through the top eye as well as the bottom eye and float cap. This float will not catch in the weeds, should a carp run into them, and have to be brought back through them. With the orthodox method of fixing a float, weed is liable to be caught between the line and float, where it is attached by the float cap. This of course does not happen if attached only by the bottom ring as in the method described.

FLOAT LEDGERING

For the angler who insists on using a float – and some anglers have no confidence if they are not, and consequently it is better for them to use one – if one wishes to cast farther than the previous method will allow (always providing he can see a float at that distance, unless he is a poor caster) he will have to resort to the running float ledger.

The tackle required for this method consists of a float and a small paternoster lead, which is stopped by a split shot 3 or 4 ft from the lead. The porcupine quill is as good as any other float for this purpose – providing it can be seen. In shallow water, it is better to have the float lying flat on the water, so that at least a couple of yards of line is between the running lead and the float. This will give the angler a chance to strike a fast-moving fish before the float is drawn with a bang up against the lead. As will be seen, the strike must be much quicker than in other methods, as a fish cannot run off as he likes, with just the drag of a line or small float. A carp will not tow along a lead, like a pike.

SURFACE FISHING FOR CARP

Fishing with a floating crust for carp, where they can be seen basking near the surface, or slowly cruising along just beneath the surface apparently without reason or interest, that is when carp can be at the most maddening to the angler. Usually, a hot day will bring about this state of affairs, but towards evening, as the water temperature drops, the crust floating on the surface will become a centre of interest. The carp seem very wary of the crust, however – probably the floating line scares them. They are like trout rising short at a fly, they swirl around the crust, and break it up, taking the pieces that break away.

If other crusts can be drifted out to them, they may become less wary and take the crusts more boldly, until the angler sees his particular crust disappear from view, followed by a great swirl, as with the line fast disappearing he sets the hook. The difficulty of fishing this method is keeping the crust on the hook for any length of time. I find that a crust from a really new loaf will last longer. To add weight for casting, if the crust is dipped for a second or two in water – after it is hooked on – the amount of water absorbed by it will give sufficient weight to cast a fair distance.

Another way of casting out is to use a balsa float. This is attached to the line at each end of the float by a rubber ring, and lies flat on the water. The farther away from the bait that it can be attached, without making it too difficult to cast, the better. The splash caused by this contraption does not help allay the suspicions of the fish, and it should only be used when the fish are too far away to get at by any other means.

Where there are bays, or corners, of the water one is fishing in which the carp can be seen near the surface, the bait can be presented to them with the help of a friend. He holds the baited hook on one side of the bay and the angler creeps round to the opposite side letting out line as he goes, but keeping it tight so as to make sure it does not drag on the surface of the water. When he almost has the carp between himself and his friend, he gently lowers the line onto the surface. His friend places the bait in the water and the angler gradually retrieves line – *as slowly as possible*. As the bait is drawn towards the fish, the angler can place it directly over them by moving farther round the bank. This method is the quietest way of presenting bait to carp, that are not close to the bank, and I have found that if not rushed at all, the carp take no notice at all of the line moving *slowly* over the water.

When carp are *feeding* on the surface, among lilies and other floating leaved water plants, there is more chance of catching them. A bait that can be placed beside a patch of these plants has a fair chance of being taken. A fairly strong line must be used, as the carp will need to be turned from the plants as soon as he is hooked.

MARGIN FISHING

Mr Richard Walker of the Carp Catchers' Club has within the past twenty years developed this method of fishing, and I think it is probably correct to say that it is the one way of surface fishing with a crust that will consistently bring results. Late evening, during the night, and early morning, are the times to try this method but carp have been taken by it during the day. On some waters, the carp love to rove along in the edges, and along the rushes, looking for various forms of food. In well-fished waters, when other anglers have gone home, and all is quiet, they have learned that many an easily come-by meal is to be had by roaming round the edges. Here they find a few crusts – the remains of someone's bait, a little farther, a few more crusts – the remains of someone's sandwiches. All this unintentional surface baiting and groundbaiting has helped to educate the fish to form this habit of bank feeding.

At night, they can be heard like noisy pigs – slop, slop, slop, then quiet. Again the sucking breaks out, a little nearer this time. The angler's heart is pounding as he sees large ripples rolling away, with their centre not far away – then again all is quiet. The expectant angler suddenly half hears, half sees, his line rustling through the rod rings. He does not know whether he heard a crust sucked into the fish's mouth or not, as he responds with a fearful strike. A curse may be heard as the rod bends for a second, and then whips the hook straight back past his ear, for it has not taken hold. Alternatively, a gasp of 'Got you, you—', as with steady hands, but trembling heart, the angler wonders at the power of the creature, that speeds towards the centre of the lake making the rod bend double and the reel sing, as if they were having no effect at all, 'It's only a 10– or 12–pounder,' he says to his friend, but secretly he is wondering 'The way this is fighting it must be a 20-pounder.' Margin fishing at night can be one of the most tensing forms of carp fishing.

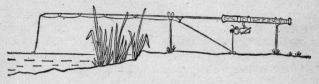

Figure 30

The manner in which the crust is fished is exceedingly simple. A rod rest is pushed in the bank, in such a fashion that the rod, resting in it, will project with its tip immediately above the position at which it is wished to fish the crust. The hook is threaded into the outside of the crust which is lowered onto the water making sure that *no* line rests on the water (Figure 30). The pick-up arm is left open and a stick placed across the line, or a couple of loops of line is pulled off the reel. The strike should take place almost immediately and I usually count 'One, two, three', bang.

One disadvantage is that it is absolutely essential the angler must be as quiet as is humanly possible, and not cause any unnecessary vibrations, as it is merely the length of his rod that decides how near to him the carp must come to take the bait. Another is that it can only be used really successfully during very warm weather, when the water is calm and there is no wind. Small roach and rudd attacking the bait on some waters can be a positive nuisance. This latter disadvantage applies to other forms of surface fishing as well as margin fishing.

Before we entirely leave the subject of margin fishing for carp, I have often thought that I would like to try to catch the carp that feed right in the bankside where there are hardly any reeds or cover. I have caught carp in such swims, but without

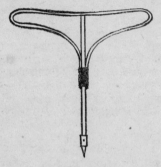

Figure 31

any cover it does not seem one is able to keep quiet enough to convince the carp that one is not present. Having tried laying my line along the grass from my rod, which was placed in a couple of rod rests approximately 15 ft from the water's edge, with a fair amount of 'bites', but having failed to hook any of them – presumably owing to the drag of the line – I have decided to try a new method next season. Incidentally, the bites I had occurred with a few inches of line *on* the water.

The tackle required for this sort of margin fishing is exactly the same as in the normal manner, except for a special kind of rod-come-line rest, as shown in Figure 31. My idea is that the line can be so arranged as to be taken by a fish without drag even though the angler is sitting back from the water some 20 ft or so (Figure 32). It will be solely the weight of the line that has to be lifted, and I would use monofilament which is very light. An immediate strike as the line tightened should hook the fish. If it swam to the left or right the line should slip off the 'line rest' without catching in it, and this should cause no inconvenience to the playing of any hooked fish. The angler would, of course, walk towards the water's edge taking line – or giving line – to get to better grips with his quarry.

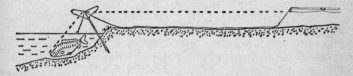

Figure 32

RE-BAITING

In surface fishing, the bait is often needed to be renewed frequently, and if small fish are present, more frequently. With margin fishing, the small fish menace can be to some extent overcome by lifting the bait just clear of the surface of the water. The bait is lowered when a carp is thought to be in the vicinity, and this is often advertised by the small fish stopping feeding on the crusts that have been thrown in to create an interest in the vicinity of the bait.

Re-baiting where there are no small fish, should not be done more frequently than every couple of hours. With a potato or worm, it is not necessary to check the bait at all, unless one has some fear of it having been thrown off during the cast.

CARP BITES AND STRIKES

For any angler who has not had the good fortune to have a carp take his bait, he will probably be amazed to see the speed at which the line runs out when it does. If using the fixed spool reel, one will see the line tearing off the spool at an alarming rate, and this type of run is not very hard to strike. I usually pick up my rod immediately, have a quick check that all is well, hold the rod at an angle of about 45 degrees in the direction of the line and after waiting until I think the time is right to strike, I slam in the pick-up. (The question of the right time to strike only comes with experience, and one cannot be told, except when there is a limit to the amount of line that can be taken by a fish.) After having picked up the line, wait until one feels the fish pulling down the rod, then give a hard pull parallel with the water.

A parallel strike is always better than an upwards one, as it is surprising how hard the roof of a carp's mouth can be.

With a fast bite, using the centre-pin or other reels, one picks up the rod and strikes when the last coil of line has gone, and the rod is being pulled down.

I rather think these fast bites are due to the line touching the fish and scaring him so that he bolts. I have noticed that it is usually when the fish is running away from one that they occur. The line would be laying alongside the fish in this case. When a fish runs to the left or right the run is often slower and the line would not necessarily be touching the fish.

A slow run, which means that the fish has taken the bait without fear, is treated in the same way as the fast run providing it is a steady run, but sometimes the fish that takes a bait slowly stops running for some reason. When this happens I pull gently on the line and if I feel something solid at the other end I strike. Ninety-nine per cent of the time it is a fish, but occasionally the carp has left the bait – or baitless hook – in the middle of a weed bed. If a fish has left the bait, it will of course come in easily when one gently pulls the line.

Another sort of run, which often may be unknown after dark until the carp reverses direction, is when the fish swims towards one. This can be seen by the line slackening. Striking this can be tricky. One waits a little while to see if the fish runs in another direction which would take line, but failing this, carefully winding up line until the carp is felt, and then an immediate strike will sometimes connect. The carp running towards one will mean that one is tending to strike the hook out of the carp's mouth instead of into it.

There are times when one just cannot hit a fish, or each one hooked soon manages to rid itself of the ironmongery. On these occasions one should check that the hook points are sharp and not blunt or bent. The bait being too hard will also arrest the penetration of the hook. Other than these causes, the poor misguided angler does come across times when he just cannot hook or land a fish. He is completely off form, and even though he does things to the letter, he does not land a fish. Such times are inexplicable but occur to the best of anglers.

PLAYING CARP

Once a carp has been hooked, it needs a cool head and a responsive pair of hands to land it. If the carp is hooked in shallow water, the long fast runs, and terrific pulling power will delight – or frighten – the angler. When these runs occur, if towards snag-free water, the fish should be allowed to run, as once in the open the task of playing them is greatly simplified.

Once in the open water, pressure can be applied to the full, by braking the edge of the reel drum with the fingers. I presume that the angler has already slipped on the check of the reel, if not a fixed spool reel. The full power of the rod is obtained by keeping the butt at approximately right angles to the direction of line. If held too high the power of the rod is wasted, as only the tip will do the work then. If the open water is deep, the carp will keep well down and bore. This is the easiest way to play a large fish, for if it can be made to keep on the move, as it swims from left to right, it can easily be turned by sidestrain from right to left, and the fight becomes a matter of keeping up fair pressure and following the fish, backwards and forwards, round and round, until it can be felt to be giving up, when the pressure can be increased to get him off the bottom.

With shallow open water the fish will not resort to these tactics, but once turned, will go hell-for-leather for the nearest weed bed. If there is plenty of room the angler may wish to let the carp run until near the danger area, so as to get the fish to tire itself, but personally – even in open water – I prefer to make the fish fight hard for every inch of line it gets.

A fish dangerously near a snag, may be turned in various ways. The rod should be laid parallel to the water and pressure on the reel drum increased until it is turned or other tactics need to be resorted to. One may move along the bank in the direction of the fish until the angle of line to the fish is such that increased pressure will turn its head, or one may get a friend to throw stones or splash about in front of the fish to scare it off its objective. If the fish reaches very soft weed, one can carry on playing it as if the weed wasn't there. If *slightly* tougher sort of weed, I do not mind a fish getting into it, as trying to swim through it, plus the full pressure the angler is applying, usually stops the carp, before it is in far enough to do much harm. I have found that when the fish stops, if one walks along the bank, taking or giving line as the case may be, and then applies the pressure from a different angle, one will turn the fish round (unless enormous), and when it moves off again it will free itself.

If the rod is not tough enough, or the fish is too large to turn by it, one must resort to hand-lining. One points the rod at the fish and, holding the line with the other hand, pulls. One may feel the fish giving, and when it does, up goes the rod into play again. The types of water plants that I do not like a fish to reach, as it often means a break, are the thick-stemmed tough plants like water-lilies, reeds, rushes, etc. With the latter two, if the rod is held very high, the line *may* pass over them and it *may* be possible to get the fish out. If deep in the former, it's 'Goodbye'.

It should not be forgotten that moving along the bank is often an excellent way of shortening the distance between oneself and the fish, thus taking up line as one goes. Playing a fish on a short line is far easier, and one has much greater control over the fish's movements, than with yards and yards of line out. Besides, if in the dark, one is more aware of the whereabouts of the fish on a short line.

In between the rushes of the fish, line can be taken by the method known as 'pumping', and I like this method equally well for fixed spool or centre-pin type reels. The line is wound in as the rod is lowered, until there is slightly more than 90 degrees between the line and the rod top. (Do not point the rod at the fish.) Then, without giving line, the rod is gradually drawn up, until it has passed through an arc of some 45 degrees, thus drawing the fish a few feet nearer. This process is repeated as often as necessary, until the fish is drawn over the net, but in the meantime should the fish tear off again, the finger eases off the reel drum, thus allowing the fish to take line. When its run is over 'pumping' can be recommenced.

If a fish splashes about on the surface, or jumps, or rolls on the surface, as they often do when hooked in shallow water, pressure should be eased, for a good wallop of the tail on a tight line might have serious results.

I must admit that during the playing of a carp I am calm enough, but directly I have landed it I shiver with the nervous tension of the battle. Although I have landed a good many double-figure fish, I cannot get over this jelly-feeling once the fish is mine.

NETTING A CARP

It is very comforting when one has hooked and played out a good carp, to know that one's friend is always capable of landing it without hitch. The number of fish lost at the net by over-excited 'netters', must run into a considerable amount.

Once a carp is nearly played out, and the rod-man knows that, apart from bad luck, the fish is his, the net should be placed into the water at the selected landing place. I always like to place my net as flat as possible against the under-water bank or bottom, so that there is no fear of the fish fouling it, should it make a last dash towards the bank, before it is completely beaten. When a fish is beaten it lays on its side and can be drawn over the net, which should be sufficiently beneath the surface to allow this. The net is lifted to engulf the fish, and the rod point can be lowered or the rod put down if two hands are needed to the net. The hand should be slid down the handle to grasp the net ring or the net meshes when the whole lot can be lifted out. It is wise to take the fish well away from the water before removing it from the net, for hook removal, photographing and so on.

The reason for a light net when one is netting one's own fish, speaks for itself. Managing a large fish with one hand, and trying to net it with a heavy, unwieldy net with the other hand is liable to cause vehement mutterings.

NIGHT FISHING

To be successful at night fishing, one must have a good knowledge of the water one is fishing, one must know all the snags, the weeds, the bankside and be prepared to find that however efficient their angling may be in the light, it can be very bad in the dark. Casting accurately, playing the fish, many things are more difficult at night than during the day.

All the things needed for the night's fishing must be arranged at hand, easy to find, but well placed, so that one is not likely to fall over, or step on, anything. If possible one should choose a swim from which one can play a fish without having to move about too much, although, once one becomes accustomed to the dark, it is surprising how clearly one can see.

One of the essentials of night fishing is comfort, and once I have arranged everything satisfactorily I settle myself into one of those small deckchair type of seats – very low, built with a metal frame. My rod is to my right, within easy reach to pick up and strike. I try to arrange things so that I can do everything without leaving my seat. On cold nights I wrap a blanket around myself and I always wear extra pullovers at night.

Once all is ready, the bait has been cast out and the line checked or sunk, it remains to detect a bite. There are various ways of accomplishing this. The old method was to place a piece of folded silver paper across the line which was lifted and moved forward by a taking fish. The line then runs through the silver paper until the fish is struck. Although this can be easily seen, and the line running through it can be heard rustling on calm nights, I am not fond of this method, as there is a slight drag. The method I favour is the stick method mentioned before. For night fishing I paint the stick black. It is rounded and smoothed, about 5 ins long, 3/16 inch in diameter. This is placed across the line at right angles to the rod, slightly off centre, so that should a fish move it slowly while the angler was not looking he could see it had been moved to another angle. Underneath is a white cloth, which shows up the stick admirably.

The electric bite-alarm or 'buzzer' consists of a small box with a wire protruding called an 'antenna'. The line is passed around this. The box is fixed to the rod rest with the antenna slightly off centre, so that the line running through the rings moves the wire inwards. This action makes contact inside the box which completes a circuit and causes the buzzer to 'buzz'.

They have an adjustment that allows them to be set so fine, that if one breathes too heavily in the vicinity they will buzz. There is no doubt, however, that they do relieve one of the tension of watching a stick, or silver paper, for hours in the dark.

Upon hooking a carp, one will find that the playing of it is difficult compared with during the day. It is hard to tell exactly where the fish is, although watching the curve of the rod against the sky will help tell one the general direction. Always shorten line whenever possible, as once you have a fish near, you can usually see where it is by the swirls. Landing the fish can be done (without the aid of a torch) with a large net, but should one think there is an exceptionally large carp on, a powerful torch can be a great help. A smaller shaded torch will help one to bait up and perform any other generalities.

It is just as essential to keep quiet and not scare the fish as during the day-time, and the angler must not think he is going to catch dozens of carp. One has blank nights, but at least one knows that one is fishing at the *right time*.

CRUCIAN CARP

This little fish can be caught by many of the methods used for roach fishing. He is an accommodating fellow who will feed well sometimes during the day, and one can take a net full of them when they are on the feed.

Baits
Crucian carp are not too fussy in their choice of bait and there is a fair list of baits that will catch them. They should not be too large as one is dealing with a species of which a 2-pounder is a good one. Paste, bread cubes, gentles, worms, various forms of grubs, almost any insect will take crucians, and I once saw a small one rising steadily to flies.

To groundbait for them, I use a cloud, as in roach-fishing, and if I am using gentles for hookbait I throw a small quantity of gentles in the swim occasionally. Once a shoal of crucians are on feed and in the swim, I find a cloud groundbait quite sufficient to keep them around and feeding.

Tackle
A 12-ft general-purpose rod with a split cane top, an ordinary centre-pin reel with a line of about 3 lb breaking strain is strong enough tackle to land most crucian in most waters. I find the ever-useful porcupine quill the best float to use, with the shot just off the bottom, but the bait laying on the bottom. It is very sensitive and very necessary, with the dithering bites of crucian carp.

The size 10 or 12 hook will accommodate the couple of gentles, or piece of paste, needed to tempt the fish. Eyed hooks can be used, but with small hooks I always prefer the neatly whipped shop hooks, providing they are a good brand.

The bites of crucian when really on feed are easy enough to strike. The float gives a bob or two and then sails merrily away when an answering strike will usually be rewarded. When they are not biting boldly, however, they can cause every known movement to the float. Sometimes the float vibrates very fast up and down, but with such a little movement that apart from the slight rippling it could hardly be seen. Other times it lays flat, dips, does all manner of things and then when one strikes one misses. If one waits long enough though it will often sink down sufficiently to cause the angler to strike and then the fish is hooked.

It is a fine little fighter, but swims in such a way that one can nearly always tell that one has hooked a crucian even before it is seen. The fish seems to wag its tail from side to side very fast, but not very far, so that one can feel the fish the other end jerking along, instead of swimming smoothly. A crucian of a couple of pounds or so will give one a couple of minutes or more of fun, and on a warm evening, in a small pond, some of which abound in crucians, there are many less pleasant ways of spending the evening than catching a few of these small, but gallant, members of the carp family.

HARRY BROTHERTON

Tench
(For identification, see Appendix I)

INTRODUCTORY

Six hundred years ago the author of *The Treatyse* wrote: 'A Tench is a good fish: and healeth all manner of other fish that be hurt if they may come to him.' The belief that a tench's slime has curative powers has been dimmed though not extinguished in the draught of modern scientific knowledge, but the tench remains 'a good fish'.

It is good on the table. Until modern transport facilities brought sea fish to every town and village there were thousands of people who, like Parson Woodforde, netted their tench ponds whenever they expected honoured company to dinner. But from an angler's viewpoint the essential goodness of tench lies in the sport it gives; for its solid, large-finned body enables it to put up resistance that demands all an angler's skill if it is to be brought to the landing net from its weed-ridden home.

Weed – if I may use that derogatory word to cover a multitude of aquatic plants – is intimately connected with tench. In the depths of its heaviest growths these fish live and feed, disliking open expanses and well-scoured channels. Their choice of habitat has given the larger and stronger specimens comparative immunity from anglers for generations, but modern tackle and methods are steadily accounting for more and more big tench.

Tench do not often fall to the angler who is one of many lining the bank of river, canal or pond. They are caught by lone anglers or those who fish with two or three quiet companions. It is in the first faint light of dawn, at dusk and in darkness that the tench angler is most likely to succeed, and on this account such anglers see much that is hidden from those who keep to civilization's conventional hours, and they have much to remember besides the catching of fish.

Why, I do not know, but as a quarry the tench has never been a popular choice among anglers. Even Walton did not waste much time over him. In his *Compleat Angler* he dismisses the tench with a mere page or two, pleading that it was 'a fish he had not often angled for'.

We meet roach specialists, pike enthusiasts, bream experts, carp 'addicts' and so on. But rarely do we meet a real tench specialist. Those we do meet are usually anglers who live within easy reach of waters famed for large and numerous tench. The average angler, he who fishes the ordinary 'run-of-the-mill' waters which contain something of everything and nothing very special of anything, rarely fishes specifically for this species. It is usually regarded as a welcome interloper who comes along occasionally to add zest to a day's roach, bream or carp fishing. Yet the odds are that in many cases the tench are the only worthwhile fish, as regards size, that these very ordinary waters hold.

Why is it that the tench is so rarely the average angler's premier quarry? The answer is, I think, that tench fishing is, at times, an uncertain business. There are few fish whose capture presents such a clearly defined and apparently easily solved problem. Yet when the tench is not inclined to cooperate few fish are harder to catch! In no other branch of coarse fishing is there such an ever-present possibility of a blank, fishless day. Tench are capricious, fickle, temperamental – call it what you will. For varying periods they will studiously ignore the angler's lures until he begins to wonder if there *are* any tench *in* the water. Then comes a day when they will feed with an abandon which makes the gluttonous perch seem fastidious by comparison. It is the ever-present possibility of these 'red-letter' days which makes tench fishing such a fascinating pursuit.

TENCH

There are two kinds of tench, the green and the golden varieties, but as the golden tench is more of an ornamental fish and is comparatively rare it is the green common tench which is of interest to anglers.

The Common Tench (*Tinca tinca*) is a fish of very distinctive appearance and is easily identified. Roach are often confused with rudd, small chub are sometimes mistaken for dace and a large gudgeon is not unlike a small barbel. But there is no doubt about the tench. A tench is a tench and once seen there is little likelihood of it being mistaken for any other species.

In the water, on those rare occasions when they can be seen, the tench looks a grey, drab creature, but out of its native element it is not really unhandsome. The blackish green of its back merges into a greyish green, shot with gold on its flanks, and its tiny closely spaced scales and neatly rounded fins give it a sleek and rather attractive appearance.

PROTECTIVE COLOURING

We can learn much about the tench and its way of life merely by examining its physical details. For instance, its very coloration tells us that it is not a dashing creature of the sunlit surface. Its colour scheme is ideal camouflage for a shy, retiring fish which seeks to lead a leisurely existence, secure and unseen, amid the mud and weed of semi-stagnant water. The natural camouflage of the tench is remarkable. From behind cover I have tossed a few maggots into still, clear water where tench were feeding. I have watched the maggots vanish, one at a time, from the bottom, with just an occasional suspicion of a grey shadow to explain their mysterious disappearance.

This camouflage is all-important to tench, which are, by nature, sluggish, lethargic creatures. For long periods they are inactive, hugging the mud of the bottom or hovering among the weeds, almost torpid, with just their protective colouring to protect them from their natural enemies. The chief one is probably the predatory pike, which *will* devour tench when driven by hunger, despite a still widely held belief to the contrary.

FEEDING HABITS

It is impossible to trace a set pattern in the feeding habits of tench, for that notoriously fickle creature can be relied upon to confound anyone who had the temerity to attempt to do so. It is possible, however, to generalize and determine when, as a rule, the angler's chances of success will be greatest.

Normally tench are timid, cautious feeders and do not generally bestir themselves to forage until the failing light of the evening gives them a sense of security. They are not, however, strictly nocturnal feeders. At times they will feed quite freely at intervals throughout the day and, strangely enough, the darkest hours of the night are not the most profitable from the angler's point of view.

At one time I often fished through the night, in the belief that it was during the hours of darkness that the tench did most of their feeding. Results did not bear out that belief. Almost always there was a blank period during the darkest hours. If the tench were feeding at all they fed through the twilight and perhaps during the first hour or so of darkness, then there would be no more bites until the dawn was approaching. This pattern was so consistent that I gave up all-night fishing altogether, and I now confine my tench fishing to the traditional and, I think, most profitable tench-fishing times. These are the twilight and the first hour of darkness, and, best of all, the hour preceding dawn and the first hours of daylight.

This rule is not, of course, infallible. At times tench have an exasperating habit of defying all rules. I have started fishing at 3 AM and sat for six hours without a single bite, then at about nine, just when I have been about to call it a day, the tench have made their belated appearance and fed freely for a couple of hours. I still remember that the very first tench I ever caught was taken in the middle of a blazing hot afternoon. Taken on the whole, however, daytime tench fishing is not a very profitable occupation. The traditional times hold most promise.

The clue to the tench's sometimes irrational feeding habits lies, I think, in its extreme susceptibility to climatic conditions. For instance, rarely will tench feed when the water is cold, below, say, 13°C (55°F). On the other hand, exceptionally hot weather also has an adverse effect on sport. Tench seem to feed freely only within fairly narrow water temperature limits.

Cautious though they are, when tench do decide to feed they feed liberally, probably to make up for their periods of abstention. Their food consists of certain vegetable matter, worms, water snails and beetles and the larval form of all kinds of aquatic insects, augmented, of course, by bread and other 'feed' introduced by hopeful anglers. Their role in nature's scheme of things seems to be that of scavengers, performing the useful function of disposing of matter which might decay and foul the water. They are, in fact, introduced into fish-ponds specifically for this purpose on the Continent where fish are bred for table purposes.

The tench's leathery mouth, ideally shaped for sucking and equipped with a barbel or 'feeler' at each corner, betrays it as a bottom feeder which grubs for its food among the mud, dead leaves and sticks which litter the bottom. Some of its food it finds clinging to the higher weed and it will sometimes rise to take matter falling through the water, but, the bulk of it is rooted up from the bed and it is there that the angler will usually find them.

Its liking for warm humid weather and its intense dislike for the cold make the tench essentially a fish of the summer. A few odd tench are taken during the winter months but, strictly speaking, the season for successful tench fishing can be narrowed down to the months of June, July, August and September; July and August being, in my opinion, the most promising period.

HIBERNATION

With the advent of the autumn and the falling of the water temperature the tench become noticeably less inclined to feed, until finally, usually some time in October, they seem to go into more or less complete hibernation for the winter.

Whether this hibernation continues unbroken throughout the winter has always been a matter for controversy. Some maintain that a warm spell in winter will reawaken them and set them foraging for food, to resume their hibernation with the return of cold weather. This may be so to a limited extent in rivers, but it is my opinion that in still water, the tench's true habitat, hibernation remains unbroken until the spring. Fishing for tench after October is likely to prove a very unrewarding occupation, although I have known them to feed quite ravenously during late September, and under very unfavourable weather conditions. I often wonder if they sense the approach of winter and have one last fling, irrespective of weather conditions, to 'stock up' for the winter fast.

In the summer, during their frequent torpid spells, tench are more or less oblivious to what is going on around them, but during the winter hibernation this oblivion becomes complete. The completeness of their hibernation is such that on occasion dormant tench have actually been lifted from the water without disturbing them. Nothing less than a sharp rap with a stick would rouse them from their stupor.

The popular supposition that tench *bury* themselves in the mud during the winter is rather an exaggeration. What happens is this: With their broad tails and big scoop-like fins they fan the bottom and displace the mud, settling among it. The displaced mud settles over them and with the coming of winter dead leaves and debris of the falling weed-growth completes their concealment. There they may lie in a state of suspended animation, concealed from the hungry pike.

SPORTING QUALITIES

It would seem from the foregoing that the tench is a rather dull creature not worthy of the angler's attention, but this is certainly not so. A tench sheds its lethargy with a vengeance the moment it feels the hook, and if it happens to be a big one the angler will have to shed his lethargy too, and quickly, if he expects to land the fish. Nor will he get it out in a hurry. He will not need the net the first time that dark-green back breaks the surface, and if it is hooked in typical tench water there will be many heart-flutterings before it comes ashore.

But first the angler has to get his tench on the hook, which normally is no mean accomplishment. On rare occasions tench will take a bait with the gay abandon of an immature perch, but normally they are shy, wily fish, whose capture demands all the skill of the angler.

SPAWNING

In spawning, tench are just as unpredictable as they are in other matters. Tench have been found full of spawn as early as May and as late as August. It is likely that spawning is not general at one period, but occurs spasmodically over an appreciable length of time, much longer than with most species of coarse fish.

With tench spawning is not a pairing or mating affair. The shoals, which usually average thirty to forty individuals, move into the weedy shallows where the females shed their eggs on to the weed growth; two or even four males fertilizing the eggs of some individual females while the eggs of others will perhaps go unfertilized.

Of the two sexes the male is normally the bigger fish and in the average shoal they outnumber the females by two or three to one. The male can be distinguished by its grosser build, its ventral fins being larger than those of the female, and of a more spoon-like or 'cockle-shell' shape.

One female may produce anything up to 300,000 eggs, which are shed spasmodically and which adhere to the weeds. Despite this great number of eggs the tench is not really a prolific breeder, at least, not on the same scale as some species. As is the case with those species whose eggs are shed casually on to weed growth there is an enormous wastage due to spawn being consumed by fish and other creatures. Only a fraction of the great number of eggs ever hatches and fewer still reach maturity.

GROWTH

How fast and how big do tench grow? This is an interesting question from the angler's point of view, but one to which little organized research has been devoted.

On the Continent tench up to 17 lb are reputed to have been bred in fish-ponds but as these were presumably artificially fed this cannot be regarded as natural growth. The largest tench caught on rod and line in Britain as at January 1972 was one of 9 lb 1 oz.

An Essex angler, to whom I am indebted for his cooperation, made observations on the growth of tench newly introduced into a southern river, while I made parallel investigations in Cheshire. Our findings were comparable. We found that the tench of 2 or 3 oz (first-year fish) gained 6 to 7 oz in the second year, roughly the same in the third year and rather more, about 9 oz in the fourth year.

Naturally growth will vary widely according to the quality of the water and it is difficult to arrive at an average growth rate, but my collaborator and I arrived at a rough weight for age scale based on observations in very ordinary waters. Here it is:

> First year – 2 to 3 oz
> Second year – 9 to 10 oz
> Third year – 1 lb
> Fourth year – 1½ lb
> Fifth year – 2 lb

The tench probably begin to spawn at this age and weight.

They would take seven or eight years to attain 3 lb and about ten years to reach 4 lb.

In really good tench water, large well-weeded lakes, these figures would, of course, be greatly exceeded. Generally speaking, large waters yield the largest tench. Large fish are rarely found in small ponds, but most waters will yield tench of a useful size, even where other species are stunted and of no account for sporting purposes. I have taken tench of from 1 to 2 lb from waters which never yielded a roach or perch of more than 4 oz. That is one very favourable point about tench fishing. When one does catch them they are almost always worthwhile fish.

Well-weeded canals have produced some notable tench.

DISTRIBUTION

The fact that they rarely catch tench in the course of their general fishing leads many anglers to think that tench are not very plentiful. One of the main reasons why many anglers do not make the tench's acquaintance is that they do not fish in the right places. Actually the tench is fairly well represented in British freshwaters.

They are present in suitable waters throughout England, parts of Wales and Ireland, and in Scotland as far north as Loch Lomond. They are most numerous in the southern, central and eastern counties of England, particularly in East Anglia and the Fen district, becoming less numerous in the northern counties. They are, however, present in numbers sufficient to justify fishing for them as far north, at least, as Lancashire and Yorkshire.

TYPE OF WATER

They are not found, however, in all classes of water. Our little study of the tench's way of life suggests the type of water where they are likely to be found. They are primarily still-water fish, thriving best in static waters such as lakes, clay, sand and gravel pits; ponds of all kinds; in fact, in any form of enclosed water excepting, perhaps, lakes with hard, rocky bottoms. Canals, too, particularly weed-grown derelict ones, usually hold a quota of tench, and so also do sluggish rivers and broads. The only waters really unsuitable for tench are strong, fast-flowing rivers. Tench have no liking for fast rivers, although they do sometimes manage to exist in them if they can find a quiet backwater, out of the rush and tumble of the main stream.

TENCH HAUNTS

In most waters tench have their particular haunts. They are not, like some species, distributed more or less evenly throughout the water. Only in very small ponds can one expect to find them anywhere. In more extensive enclosed waters such as lakes, meres, flashes and large pits they make certain well-defined areas their 'headquarters' and rarely do they roam far from 'base'. In and around lily-beds, among banks of sub-surface weeds and along the rushy fringes; these are the favourite haunts of the tench. They are not, as a general rule, frequenters of deep water, preferring the shallower areas where the weed growth is more abundant. The finer kinds of weed seem to have an attraction for tench, and those areas of a water which are carpeted by this type of weed growth are always likely tench-fishing areas.

In most enclosed waters there is usually an area where the bottom is muddier than elsewhere, due to dead leaves and other floating debris being carried by the action of the prevailing winds. Such areas are always favourite haunts for mud-loving tench.

CANALS AND RIVERS

In rivers, likely tench water is not difficult to spot. One will not be far wrong by choosing any quiet, slack water out of the main current; broads, weedy lay-bys and backwaters and any silted areas being especially favourable.

Derelict, disused canals are usually well weeded all along their length and the tench will be more or less evenly distributed, but in well-navigated canals, with little weed growth, locating them is a rather more difficult proposition. In such waters trench tend to keep on the move, settling only if they find an area where food is plentiful. Most of these navigated canals have certain spots favourable for tench fishing but it is impossible to locate them without local knowledge. There are no natural features to mark these places as likely tench haunts, simply because they are not *natural* tench haunts at all. They are artificially created. This is how it happens.

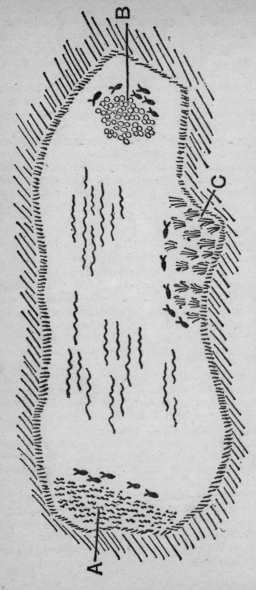

Figure 33 Sketch of typical lake showing likely tench haunts. A. Submerged weed bed. B. Water-lily beds. C. Muddy bottom with marginal weeds

At some time or other an angler makes a good catch of tench in a particular spot by having the luck to 'drop among them'. He spreads the good news and from then on that spot is fished intensively, each successive angler introducing his quota of ground bait. The tench become accustomed to finding food in this area and they linger in the vicinity. In consequence further good catches are made and the spot acquires a reputation and is rarely without a tenant. The almost continuous supply of 'feed' encourages the tench to make their home in that area.

However, these favourable tench-fishing stations are always in great demand, and if the angler has easy access to the water it would pay him to establish a good 'tench spot' of his own, one known only to himself. This can be accomplished by the very same process which makes the reputed tench swims; by regular groundbaiting.

'BLOWING' TENCH

At times feeding tench very conveniently betray their whereabouts by 'blowing', or sending up streams of tiny bubbles as they grub for food on the bottom. This 'blowing' or 'bubbling' is not peculiar to the tench; carp and bream are both well-known 'bubblers', and almost all the other bottom-feeding species produce this phenomenon at times, although to a lesser extent than the tench, carp and bream. The blowing of the tench, however, is most distinctive and unmistakable. Tench bubbles are tiny and very numerous, coming to the surface in a steady stream, sometimes lingering there for a time like a bubbly foam before finally disintegrating. Once seen they can never be mistaken for the larger isolated bubbles caused by gases released from the bottom, or the streams of larger bubbles produced by other species.

There is a difference of opinion as to the origin of these telltable bubbles. Some anglers hold that they come from the bed itself; that they are trapped gases released when the mud is disturbed by feeding fish. Others are of the opinion that the bubbles emanate from the fish themselves, from the mouth or gills. I am inclined to favour the latter theory. If the bubbles came from the mud it is logical to suppose that they would be similar whichever species was responsible for them. Tench bubbles are definitely much smaller than any others, probably due to some physical peculiarity of that species.

145

Whatever the cause tench bubbles are, at times, a valuable guide to the tench-fisher seeking the haunts of his quarry. Sometimes the observant angler will find a well-defined trail of such bubbles, in and around the weed beds, leading to the very spot where the tench are foraging. Unfortunately tench do not *always* give rise to these bubbles. Sometimes tench after tench may be taken, proving that they are feeding strongly, yet there may not be a solitary bubble in evidence. But the blowing of feeding tench is a sign always worth looking out for.

Sometimes, though not very often, tench can actually be seen, lying motionless just beneath floating weed or water-lilies. Rarely, though, can they be caught on such occasions. Basking carp can often be tempted with a floating bait, but basking tench are usually a hopeless proposition. They seem to be utterly indifferent to the angler's offerings, no matter how tempting. They do, however, pin-point the area where tench are to be found, knowledge which can be put to profitable use on more favourable occasions.

TENCH TACTICS: PRELIMINARY PREPARATION

It is possible, on occasion, to enjoy good tench fishing without any previous preparation, which is perhaps fortunate for that majority of anglers who do not have easy access to the waters they fish. If the tench water one intends to fish is two or three hours' journey away preliminary preparation is impossible and one just has to make the best of a bad job, for without a doubt a carefully prepared fishing spot increases considerably one's chances of success in the quest for tench.

Ideally it takes a week or more to thoroughly prepare a spot for tench fishing. (I use the word 'spot' because the usual term 'swim' is rather inappropriate to still-water fishing.) At least a week before the anticipated fishing date a likely tench haunt is selected, with due regard to the practicability of landing one's fish. It is of little use hooking and playing a fish only to find that it is impossible to get it out. This is where the use of a boat is invaluable. By mooring his boat in a strategical position the boat angler can fish water which is absolutely impracticable to the bank fisher.

If the chosen spot is typical tench water some preliminary clearing will almost certainly be necessary before pre-baiting is commenced. A certain amount of marginal weed may have to be cleared to make an avenue along which any possible captures can be brought to the net. This clearing of marginal weed should not, however, be too drastic, as it is destroying valuable cover.

The bottom should be cleared of weed growth which might obscure the bait. If a boat is available and if the water is not too deep this operation can be performed with an ordinary garden rake, but in the absence of a boat it may be necessary to improvise a 'drag' by festooning a length of barbed wire about

Figure 34 Weed drag improvised from iron bar and length of barbed wire

some heavy object and attaching to it a clothes line (Figure 34). This drag is thrown out and drawn across the bed repeatedly, working progressively across the fishing area until a patch some 6 yds square is made reasonably clear of weed growth. Having made the place fishable the next step is to encourage the fish to feed in the cleared area by the regular introduction of groundbait.

Each day an amount of well-soaked bread groundbait is thrown in, with a quota of maggots or chopped-up worms intermixed, the choice depending upon which is intended to be used as hook bait. Although they are liberal feeders tench are not so gluttonous as the bream, for instance, so it is not wise to *over*-feed them. Four or five good handfuls should be enough at the start and this amount should be gradually reduced to about two handfuls on the day prior to fishing. If this procedure is conscientiously carried out there is a good chance of finding foraging tench in the prepared area on the actual fishing date, unless, of course, it happens to be one of the tench's many 'off' days.

It is unwise to throw further groundbait into the area immediately before commencing to fish, for it may put down tench already feeding there. It pays to fish for half an hour or so and then, if there is no activity, a small offering of bread and hook bait mixture can be introduced, but with as little disturbance to the water as possible.

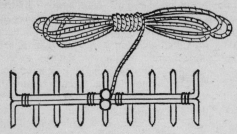

Figure 35 A more portable weed drag made from two garden-rake heads bound together

Daybreak is the ideal time to fish a newly prepared spot for the first time, for it is inadvisable to make an earlier start in the dark until one has fished the place a time or two and has become familiar with the terrain. Sometimes the tench may not begin to feed until long after daybreak and the early rising may seem in vain, but as tench are such unpredictable feeders one cannot risk 'missing the bus'.

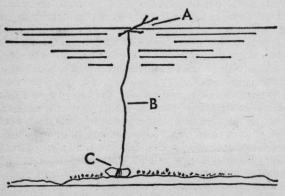

Figure 36 Device for marking exact position of ground-baited area. A. Twig. B. Cotton. C. Stone

Obviously the foregoing is tench fishing under ideal conditions, possible only when the angler has his water close at hand. How about the poor old town-dweller, who can get down to his water perhaps only once a week? If the urban angler intends to fish seriously for tench he will probably have to alter his usual fishing programme.

The average fisherman's day out is not, as a rule, very promising for good tench fishing. He gets up at a civilized hour, catches his bus, train or coach and arrives at the waterside by, say, 10 AM, by which time the tench have probably fed to repletion and are drowsing in their weedy retreats. By the time the quarry are stirring again in search of food the angler is homeward bound with an empty basket. That is half the secret of successful tench fishing; to fish at the right time.

If the angler has his own means of conveyance getting down to the water by daybreak presents no difficulty. It is just a matter of getting up early enough. If, however, he depends on public transport, the only way out is to travel down the previous evening and arrange sleeping facilities for the night, either a tent or 'bed and breakfast' at some place near by which caters for anglers. If it can be arranged, travelling down the previous evening is probably the best plan, as the angler can fish until dark and then groundbait a spot in readiness for daybreak on the morrow. Clearing of weed should not be attempted, however, so near to the time of fishing. There is no time for the tench to recover from their alarm at this drastic reorganization of their environment. The angler must seek a likely haunt which is already fishable.

The angler who makes his first arrival at daybreak can do little in the way of preparation without disturbing the fish and prejudicing his chances. All he can do is to seek a promising spot, keeping a sharp look-out for the blowing of feeding tench, fish it for half an hour or so and if sport is not forthcoming then introduce a small amount of groundbait as unobtrusively as possible. This is best done by squeezing a ball of groundbait firmly around the lead shot on the hook length, swinging it gently into the water and then shaking it off with a twitch of the rod top.

Normally tench are shy, timid creatures; not as shy as carp, perhaps, but nevertheless easily alarmed. Unnecessary movement and heavy footfalls must be avoided at all times. If fishing is being done from a boat the craft must be brought into position as quietly as possible, not too near to the fishing area, and the anchoring weights must be lowered with the utmost care.

BAIT PRESENTATION

It is normally essential to present a tench with a motionless bait. This can be achieved by ledgering or 'laying on'. Ledgering includes the straightforward method, and shot ledgering, running ledgering and ledgering with a float. All these have been discussed in earlier sections.

When the bottom has been cleared of plant growth, there is no problem. Figures 37 and 38 show two methods of fishing for tench over un-cleared ground.

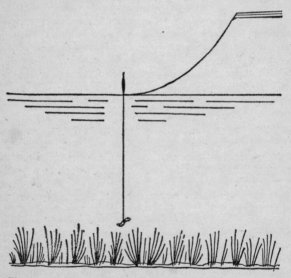

Figure 37 Fishing over un-cleared bottom. Float set to suspend bait *just* clear of weed

TENCH BITES

Once the tench does make up its mind to take the bait the bite is a very satisfying affair. With running ledger tackle the float

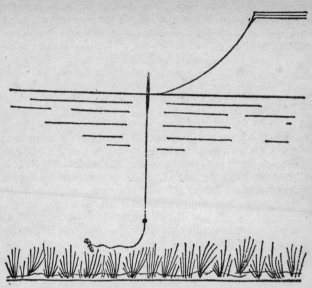

Figure 38 Fishing over un-cleared bottom 'laying on' over top of weed

just sinks from sight, slowly and majestically, giving the angler all the time in the world in which to strike. When laying on or shot-ledgering the float rises in the water, falls over flat and then glides away into the deeps at a leisurely pace. On such occasion one can pick up the rod at the first knock and then wait, striking when the float disappears from view.

At other times, however, when the tench are dubious, tench bites can be very exasperating. The float waves and dithers, creeps along a few inches, sinks until only about $\frac{1}{2}$ inch is showing, only to shoot up again in a maddening fashion just as the angler is tensed to strike. And around the float there may be streams of tiny bubbles to betray that feeding tench are responsible for its antics. As a rule it is futile to try to hit a tench when the float is behaving in this fashion. In fact, I am of the opinion that much of this float movement is not caused by tench mouthing the bait, but is caused by the bait and cast being wafted about by the broad tails of tench foraging in the vicinity.

Usually, however, a partial *sinking* of the float denotes that a fish has the bait in its mouth and in the absence of a more definite bite a snap strike will sometimes connect. Sometimes a couple of turns of the reel handle will make up the tench's mind. The sudden movement of the bait makes the fish think that it is a case of 'now or never' and often a definite bite is the result. Sometimes a change of bait may do the trick.

PLAYING AND LANDING TENCH

When the hook sinks home and the angler becomes tethered to his tench his troubles are not over by any means. There are no fancy manoeuvres about the tench's bid for liberty. To the tench weeds spell security and there it heads the moment it feels the hook. Keeping a steady pressure on the fish the angler must let it go so far, and no farther. As soon as there is a danger of the fish reaching sanctuary the angler must apply all the strain that the tackle will stand. Once it is turned the tench will probably head off towards some other weed bed or snag and the angler must be ready to take the appropriate action.

Sometimes tench have a habit of boring straight for the mud of the bottom and it is wise to keep them up from it as they have an uncanny knack of finding some snag or other to wrap the tackle around.

MARGIN FISHING

Tench can be caught by the technique described in the section on carp.

A. L. WARD

Pike (*Esox lucius*)
(*For description, see Appendix I*)

FOOD

Concerning the food of pike, John Taverner's dictum, written in the sixteenth century, puts the matter in a nutshell. 'A pike,' he writes, 'will hardly feed of anything except it stirre and be alive.' Particularly do I like that ancient author's use of the word 'hardly', for it extends its cover to those strange items which from time to time turn up in pike autopsies. For instance, on several occasions I have opened pike stomachs which contained nothing more active than masses of frog spawn. At other times food items as varied as frogs, crayfish, ducklings and other waterfowl, and – on at least one occasion – a full-grown rat have been disclosed in my investigations. They also take dead fish lying on the bottom.

It is beyond question that smaller fishes form Esox's staple diet. Not even his own kith and kin are safe when the pike is in ravenous mood, and all manner of freshwater fishes from minnow to salmon serve to fill its hungry maw. In this connexion it may be well to draw attention to a fallacy which exists to some extent even among modern pike anglers. It is sometimes stated that pike will not eat perch on account of the latter's sharp, spiny dorsal fin. Nothing could be farther from the truth since pike feed freely on perch in waters where the two species dwell together. Furthermore, perch are a popular live bait on the set-lines used in some Irish waters and have accounted for numerous pike of all sizes.

By reason of the catholic tastes exhibited by pike, it was a common belief of earlier times that pike are perpetually in a murderous humour. Whatever was true about the appetite of pike in those distant days there is no doubt that present-day pike enjoy periods of fasting as well as of feasting. And it can definitely be said in Esox's favour that it is no ruthless killer – slaughtering for the sheer lust of killing. Nature has ordained that the pike shall exist mainly on a fish diet, and this the pike does in no uncertain fashion. But the pike slays solely for the purpose of its own survival, even if at times the victim is over-large and takes some considerable time to stomach.

John Garvin's record Irish pike – a 53-pounder – had a 10-lb salmon inside it and a salmon of this weight is no small mouthful. Many other instances are on record concerning the voracity of pike. Most pike anglers of long standing will, indeed, have first-hand evidence of the appetite of pike since it is commonplace to land sizeable pike which bear wounds and scars upon their flanks as mute witness to the attacks of larger fish.

Examples of outstanding appetite are, however, apt to be misleading. All too often it is taken for granted that Esox is possessed of an unsatiable appetite and that he is perpetually seeking to fill a hungry maw. This is anything but true. Pike are as incalculable as any fish that swim – more so, indeed, than most. There are times, undoubtedly, when not one or two, but, seemingly, every pike in a particular water comes on the feed simultaneously. For me at any rate this is one of the major mysteries of pike fishing. For a time sport may be out-standing as pike after pike drives at the angler's bait with gay abandon. This strange collective action may continue for an hour or two, and it is then that record bags are on the pro-gramme.

But these are exceptional occasions, and the pike angler fortunate enough to experience one is well advised to make the most of his opportunity. In the normal course of events, pike need tempting – and for anything approaching consistent success in modern pike waters the angler will need to pay full attention to his quarry's moods and habits.

Fortunately for the sport of pike fishing, hunger is not the only incentive urging a pike to seize a bait or lure. Or so at least my personal experience tends to teach me. Time and time again I have taken pike which were apparently unin-terested in satisfying their normal appetite.

Curiosity, jealousy, anger – call it what you will! – I firmly believe that pike will on occasions strike at the angler's lure simply because that lure is behaving unnaturally and is there-fore worthy of its attention.

Mature pike are solitary in the sense that they are devoid of shoaling instincts. Under normal circumstances where several pike are gathered together in comparatively close company, it is only thus because local circumstances so ordain it. Food prospects, for instance, may be good in that particular portion of the water. Or else the fish may find the immediate surroundings particularly well suited to their mode of living. In times of flood, for instance, a number of pike may seek sanctuary in the sheltering eddies of the same backwater. In rivers where stretches of fast water alternate with deep, slow-running pools, pike will tend to concentrate in the quieter pools. Even here, however, it is usually a matter of each fish having its own separate, albeit narrow-confined, domain. For, in the main, adult pike are solitary fish, and it is only under the influence of the reproductive urge that individual fish intentionally foregather.

Not that this reproductive influence is an *immediate* harbinger of the act of spawning. Just as the spawning migrations of many sea fish species have their commencements months before the actual depositing of the eggs, so, too, do pike react to the procreative urge in their fashion some considerable time before actual spawning takes place.

Early winter may find the sexes commencing to pair. Perhaps, strictly speaking, the word 'pair' is technically incorrect since a female pike may be attended by two or even more male consorts. This attendance, moreover, is no mere casual link and the New Year pike angler may frequently take several fish from what is virtually the same patch of water.

Large pike will usually be found to be female fish. Where several pike are gathered together for spawning purposes it is highly probable that the largest fish is the female with the smaller pike playing the role of prospective suitors. It is frequently stated that during and after spawning female pike are only too eager to devour their smaller spouses. On this point I have no positive evidence, although it is by no means beyond the realms of possibility. Certainly, during spawning operations, it is customary to witness frantic scurryings to and fro in shallow water. Whether these activities result from female chasing male or vice versa, I am not in a position to say.

The time for the spawning of pike varies considerably. Egglaying may take place any time during the period from

February to April – depending upon prevailing weather conditions. Normally the early months of the year coincide with high water and flooded banks, and pike may be expected to spawn from February onwards. In times of drought, during late winter and early spring, however, spawning prospects may be considerably impaired. March and even April may find the normal spawning grounds high and dry and, strangely enough, pike will shed their ova only in suitable surroundings. Investigations on some well-known pike lakes have shown that, following an unusually dry spring, numbers of pike will remain unspawned as late as June, and such fish will frequently be found to be in the process of reabsorbing their ova.

Spawning takes place in the shallow areas of the waters involved. In the case of river pike, the shallow weed beds of the backwaters and the weedy stretches of inflowing ditches and drains are favourite situations. Lake pike deposit their eggs in the weedy shallows along the shoreline, particularly in those areas where winter floods have inundated tracts of low-lying grasslands.

When freshly laid the eggs are sticky and they adhere readily to weeds and stones in the vicinity. Vast numbers of eggs are deposited by individual fish. Frank Buckland tells of a female pike of 32 lb which was found to contain over half a million eggs. The incubation period varies somewhat with the temperature of the water, but is usually a matter of several weeks. After a further few weeks, during which period the yolk-sac of the newly hatched fry is absorbed, the rapidly growing young pike forsake the nursery shallows for the greater safety of the reed beds.

During the first few years of their existence pike grow rapidly, and their diet is a varied one. Needless to say, much will depend on the food items available, but insect larvae, shrimps, snails and fish fry constitute the bulk of their diet. Pike normally attain maturity – ie become fit to breed – at an age of three years or thereabouts. By this time they may have acquired a weight of approximately 3 lb and will, for the most part, have become definite fish-eaters. Subsequent growth rate is dependent mainly on the quantity of food fishes available, so that waters plentifully stocked with minor fishes usually produce the heaviest pike.

It would be unwise to attempt to forecast the *maximum* weight to which pike may attain. The present record for rod-caught pike stands at 53 lb – Mr John Garvin's fish taken in 1920 from Ireland's Lough Conn. This record-breaking pike contained a partially digested salmon weighing 10 lb, and the weight of this latter was *not* included in the weight claimed for the pike. It is noteworthy that on the same day he took his

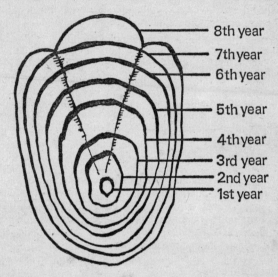

8th year
7th year
6th year
5th year
4th year
3rd year
2nd year
1st year

Figure 39 Diagrammatic sketch of pike scale from 21 lb female fish, showing growth over eight years

top-weight pike Mr Garvin also landed a 30-pounder. Angling fortune was with him, too, some twenty-odd years later, when he landed a pike of 42 lb from the same water.

Tens of thousands of words have been written in angling books and periodicals about real or mythical pike of great size. There are claims for Irish pike of 90 lb and more, and no doubt bigger pike than Mr Garvin's subsist – but none are proven. There seems no doubt that a blind and emaciated pike taken dead from a Cheltenham lake in 1896 weighed something about 60 lb, so one day the rod record may be broken. All other reports are suspect.

In general pike prefer slow-running or still waters where underwater weeds are plentiful. Rivers, canals, lakes, broads, ponds and – to a lesser extent – large gravel pits all provide suitable surroundings, particularly where the water is alkaline in character. Waters which are definitely acid are not well suited to pike. This does not, however, rule out waters in marshy or boggy terrain for these may lie over limestone or chalk strata. Indeed some of the best pike lakes in Ireland are of this nature although at first sight the visiting angler might well regard them as typically acid waters.

Underwater cover is an essential to the well-being of pike. For, although on occasion hungry pike will forage in open water, their normal mode of living is linked with the art of ambush. Lying in or near convenient cover, and motionless except for gentle, balancing movements of the fins, the pike literally waits for its meals to come to it. The smaller fishes, which figure so prominently on its menu, swim as it were into the very Jaws of Death. Unconscious of the hidden danger threatening them, the unsuspecting victims move into the pike's sphere of action – usually an area of several yards. Then – a swift lunge and a savage snap means that Esox has made yet another foray from its place of ambush.

In rivers, pike are generally to be found in the deeper, slow-flowing reaches. Particularly is this the case when higher water levels result in increased flow. In summer, for instance, when rivers are low and currents gentle, pike tend to scatter farther afield and may frequently be found lying at the edges of or actually in the modest stream. Even here, however, it will usually be found that they are not actually swimming aginst the full force of the current. Some underwater feature may well create an eddy invisible on the surface. It may be a depression in the river bed, or, perhaps, an unnoticed obstruction in the shape of boulder, weed bed, etc. Whatever the cause, it will usually be the case that Esox is expending no more energy than is necessary and, in all likelihood, is taking full advantage of some favourable underwater eddy.

During floods, when the water is high and coloured, pike are particularly prone to seek sheltered situations. Under such circumstances pike frequently undertake minor migrations and literally all the pike in a particular stretch of river may congregate in a common resting place. Backwaters and deep

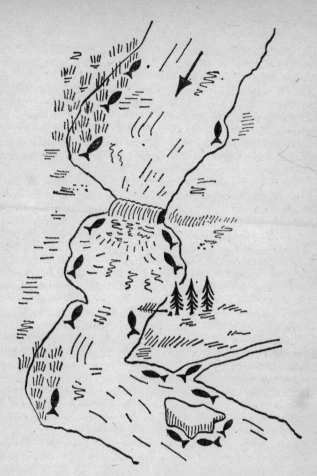

Figure 40 Diagram of likely 'lies' for river pike

slow-moving eddies provide sanctuaries of this nature and sheltering pike usually lie virtually on the bottom.

Even under normal conditions the river pike will not often be found in situations where the fish has to work hard to hold its position. For preference, pike choose as their haunts those places where the current is incapable of severely jostling a lurking fish. For this reason, the deep, slowly swirling pockets, which frequently form at the edges of the current downstream from waterfalls, weirs and sluices, are favourite lurking places for pike. So, too, are the inner sides of river bends, particularly where there is a considerable growth of underwater weed in the slack water to serve as cover. The mouths of drains – cow-drinks and the minor bays formed by outjutting banks – bridge buttresses – the tails of islands – felled trees or large branches, lying in the water – weed beds or large stones upon the river bed – these and like situations all provide conditions beloved by pike, particularly where the surrounding water carries any strength of current.

In the straight, slow-flowing river reaches pike may be more widespread. Seldom, however, will they be found in places devoid of cover. Reed-fringed banks and midstream weed beds will here provide favourite lurking places for pike as will backwaters, channels in the weed beds and similar placid situations.

In the lakes the locating of pike is a less simple matter. So many places may seem equally promising that the problem is to choose the *most* likely. Local knowledge can help considerably since, year after year, pike show preferences for particular resorts. Weedy bays – particularly those in which rudd, perch and other food fishes are known to rendezvous – provide likely water. River entrances and outflows – particularly the former – likewise are probable holding grounds, as are the vicinities of boathouse piers and jetties.

Frequently in lakes, fences extend well into the water to prevent the straying of livestock in times of low water. Where these posts are sunk in water of fair depth, their near-vicinity is always worth a trial. Minor fishes commonly frequent such situations and Esox may well be lurking near by. Where islands – even minor ones – are present in lakes, the waters adjacent to their shorelines frequently hold pike for in such localities underwater cover, in the shape of weeds, boulders and rock-formations, is usually present. By and large, however, the element of luck plays a prominent part in the fortunes of the lake angler. The area of likely water is usually so extensive that sizeable pike may be widely distributed. The angler who covers the greatest area of probable 'holding ground' is the most likely to encounter some, at least, of these scattered pike so that it is unwise for the pike angler to tarry overlong in any one locality. It is noteworthy that in early

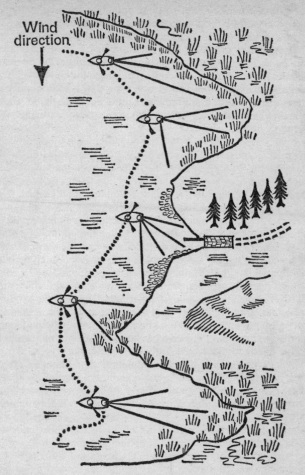

Wind direction

Figure 41 Diagram of casting technique in spinning for lake pike

morning and in late evening, pike tend to forage in the more open water and during these excursions they may be encountered at considerable distance from their daytime haunts.

Pike in canals, broads, ponds and similar still waters follow the same general pattern of distribution as that of lake pike. The absence of strong currents is the reason for the similarity since the pike in all these types of water are free to take up stations where they choose. The main factor influencing this choice is therefore, not one of physical discomfort – as is the case in rivers – but rather one of suitability as a feeding station. Still-water pike, therefore, should be sought mainly in the vicinity of underwater cover and particularly in those places which the angler's experience recognizes as likely pike haunts.

BAITS, LURES AND MISCELLANEOUS TACKLE

Accepting minor fishes as being the staple food of pike it is obvious that natural fish bait (either alive or dead) and fish-like lures will form the basis of the pike angler's armoury. For live baiting the main factor influencing the choice of a particular fish species as bait will likely be that of convenience. Where possible, however, I am a firm believer in the advisability of using a live bait to which the pike are locally accustomed. Experiments with set-lines have shown that pike discriminate even between fish species common to the locality. The introduction as bait of a species foreign to a particular water may well cause pike to be definitely suspicious. Moreover, by using baits captured locally, difficulties of transport may be largely overcome with the result that lively (as opposed to 'half-dead') baits are presented for the pike's attention.

In this connexion, it should be noted that small perch are remarkably sturdy fish. Even on live-bait tackle they remain active for long periods. Perch are, however, extremely susceptible to fungus after any kind of rough treatment and will seldom survive more than a few days if kept in stock in restricted conditions. For this reason perch are unsuitable for those anglers who are obliged to obtain their supply of live baits several days before an angling outing. For this purpose, rudd are admirably suited, since they are remarkably hardy and survive under poor conditions of captivity. Apart from the species mentioned, roach, dace, gudgeon, bream, carp, tench, small pike, minnow and, indeed, almost every species of minor freshwater fish at times figure on Esox's menu so that the live baiter should not suffer from want of variety.

For use as natural dead baits for spinning, trolling or trailing, the pike angler has an even wider selection. Preserved dead baits are added to his list as are saltwater species such as herring and whiting. It is my experience, however, that preserved baits are a poor substitute for freshly killed baits as 'pike-getters' and, where they have to be put into service, I prefer baits pickled in salt to those preserved in formalin or other chemicals. Slim, stream-lined fish spin better than deep-bellied ones and they also impose less strain on angling equipment.

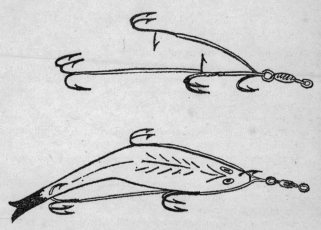

Figure 42 Mounted wobble tackle (top view)

Dead baits may be mounted either on *true* spinning tackle (such as the popular 'Archer' mount) or on wobble tackle (Figure 42) – whereby the bait revolves in a series of sweeping spirals. My own choice is for a wobbling dead bait and the wider the wobble the more I like it. The degree of wobble is regulated by the amount of curve put into the tail of the bait and the unpractised angler may have to adjust his hook flight several times before obtaining the desired effect.

In the matter of artificial spinning lures the pike angler has the choice of an almost endless variety and each season sees more new patterns appearing on the market. The majority of these lures will at times take pike, but a few proven 'killers' should form the basis of every angler's collection. The old-fashioned spoon bait (Figure 43) is a deadly pike lure provided that it works actively and that its hooking power is not impaired by undersize hooks. The addition of a bunch of longish feathers to the tail treble of a spoon often enhances its effectiveness. However, not every spoon will carry this

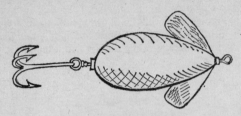

Colorado spoon bait

Eyed Norwich spoon

A lively feathered spoon. Side view

Top view

Willow-leaf bar-spoon

Figure 43

appendage without the sacrifice of action so that experiment alone should decide which lures will be thus decorated.

Wagtails (Figure 44), too, are first-class lures despite their tendency to double-back and entangle in the trace during

Figure 44 Wagtail

casting. This failing can be eliminated to a considerable extent by confining the arming to *two* treble-hooks – one at the tail and the other attached (not too flexibly) midways down the body.

Plugs (Figure 45) – especially the jointed models – have

Figure 45 Top: Solid plug. *Bottom:* Jointed plug

proved excellent on many waters and are now almost as popular in this country as they are on the other side of the Atlantic. Colorado, Kidney-bar and other bar-type spoons are also first-rate 'medicine' for pike and possess the virtue of working actively even when drawn slowly through the water (Figure 47).

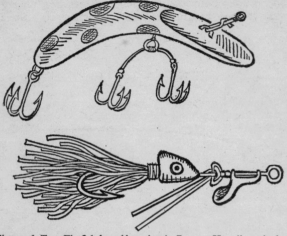

Figure 46 *Top:* Flatfish lure (American). *Bottom:* Hawaiian wiggler lure, with weedless hook (American)

Figure 47 Kidney bar-spoon

Mention has been made of but a few of the many types of pike lures. Individual anglers will have their own particular 'fancies', both in the shape of shop-bought lures and home-produced adaptions. The patterns mentioned above are, however, all popular and well-proven favourites. By all means, let the experimentally minded angler try out new models as they take his fancy, since they may also make appeal to lurking pike. In the main, however, it is in the method of working the lure – rather than in its particular pattern – that there lies the chief hope of tempting Esox from his underwater lair.

The majority of spinning lures demand the employment of a trace. Not alone is the trace an added safeguard against damage from the pike's sharp teeth, but it also serves as a connecting link between swivels. All revolving lures tend to kink the reel line unless the twists which they impart are

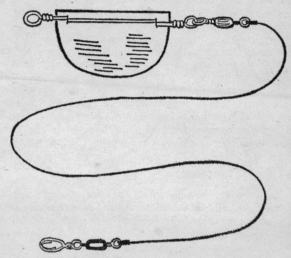

Figure 48 Spinning trace, fitted with anti-kink disc and spring-link swivel

nullified in initial stages. *Free-working* swivels at the head of the lure and also at the commencement of the trace will do much to combat line twist. Personally, I also use an 'anti-kink' device in the shape of a semicircular plastic (or celluloid) disc, incorporated into and at the head of the trace. This 'anti-kink' is thus in front of all the swivels and, acting as a keel, prevents twisting of the reel line. Anti-kink leads clipped on the line in front of the swivels or suspended from the leading eye of the front swivel serve the same purpose (Figure 48). The trace itself should be about 2 ft in length. It may be either a length of single-strand, rustless wire or else a strand of monofilament nylon. It is advisable to have this trace of a somewhat lesser breaking strain than that of the reel line so that in the event of enforced breakage through 'hang-ups', etc, the minimum of loss will follow.

Since pike claim pride of place as the leviathans among coarse fish the pike angler must fit himself out with some device for their secure landing. The gaff is the traditional weapon for this purpose and there is no denying that it is a most effective one. If, however, the sporting angler wishes to return captured fish to the water – and in the majority of cases this should be the natural desire – the gaff should *not* be used in traditional fashion – ie, by gaffing the pike in the body. Instead, the considerate angler should gaff his fish through the chin so that the point penetrates the lower jaw. This practice is by no means as difficult as it may sound since a played-out pike usually comes to the gaff with its mouth wide open. When dealing with lesser pike, the gaff may often be dispensed with and the fish landed by 'beaching' on a conveniently sloping bank, but since the good angler is always imbued with hopes of a 'big 'un', no pike angler can be deemed complete unless accompanied by his gaff.

SPINNING FOR PIKE

It can, I believe, be said without fear of contradiction that spinning for pike is the most scientific and most sporting method of pike fishing. Particularly is this the case where the angler is operating from the bank of a river. Spinning for Esox from a boat with the assistance of an adept boatman is a more simple art and one which may, on occasions, be practised on the larger rivers. In the main, however, boat fishing for pike is an affair of the lakes and similar extensive waters. Consequently, references to river fishing hereinafter should be taken as referring mainly to operations from the bank unless mention is made to the contrary.

In spinning for river pike accurate casting, knowledge of the quarry's habits and the ability to overcome obstacles all combine to make the expert angler. Without a fair degree of competence in these major qualifications the angler who seeks his river pike by spinning may well meet with disappointments. For the haunts of river pike are usually in those places least relished by the angler. Favourite 'lies' for river pike are along the edges of weed beds and in the vicinity of underwater obstructions. Tackling a sizeable pike in territory of this nature is no simple task. In many cases, the arena is limited in size by these natural 'snags' although the limits are imposed solely on the angler. The pike recognizes no such boundaries and much of its effort will be directed towards seeking safety in these nearby sanctuaries. Yet, by reason of the ambush-loving habits of his quarry, the river pike angler can ill afford to shun these threatening obstructions. To avoid them is to court disappointment. Pike are lazy fish: they prefer their meals to be served, as it were, into their laps. The lure which stands the best chance of tempting a pike is the one which literally passes by the fish's nose.

As a result accurate casting is essential to consistent success in spinning for river pike. The lure may have to be flicked under overhanging branches if it is to reach its target. It may be a matter of dropping it in a narrow laneway through weed beds or even, as in one place I know, casting the bait above a disused eel weir and guiding it accurately through the 'Queen's Gap'. For, in this particular case, time and time again, pike lay downstream of – and literally nose on to – the boundary stake and seldom were they found elsewhere in the vicinity.

Accuracy of casting, however, is but one weapon in the expert angler's armoury. Knowledge of the quarry's habits is another. Moreover this latter attribute is the directive behind the majority of casting activities. For the expert angler seldom, if ever, casts aimlessly. Each and every cast is directed so that on its return journey, the lure will pass through water wherein, angling experience tells him, a pike *might* take up quarters. The sought-after quarry may not be at home at that particular moment but, none the less, the lure has in its journey traversed 'pikey' water.

In this connexion, however, it must be emphasized that seemingly unlikely water will sometimes produce pike. Particularly is this the case where the lure has passed through a possible pike lie. For, although pike seldom pursue their *natural* food for any great distance, their behaviour towards the angler's lures is somewhat different. Perhaps curiosity vies with appetite when a spoon or wagtail comes careering in strange fashion through their field of vision. For pike will, on occasions, follow a spinning lure for a considerable distance. Most pike anglers will have first-hand experience of the spectacle of a pike thus following their lure. Looking like a miniature submarine, the pike slips into view behind the moving lure. At times, it seems to swim almost nose-on to the tail treble-hook. Frequently the fish will lunge savagely at the bait almost at the water's edge as if in fear that this strange object is about to escape. At other times suspicion will bring caution in its train. The pike may either sheer off at the last moment or else remain motionless in the water close to the angler's feet. In the latter case, if the angler makes no sudden movement to alarm his prospective victim, the pike will likely soon disappear like a shadow into the depths from whence it came.

These pike which follow the lure should always be regarded as 'possibles'. Despite their refusal to seize the bait in its initial passage, their interest has obviously been aroused. Thorough searching of the water nearby, preferably with a different lure, may well establish contact, provided the fish has not been unduly alarmed. With Esox in particularly refractory mood, it is not unusual to move him several times before he finally succumbs or else retires sulking to his sanctuary.

Both the depth and the speed at which the lure is retrieved are major factors in successful spinning. Normally pike lie deep. Their customary direction of attack is from below – upwards. If the angler's lure is to challenge a response it must come within the ken of lurking pike. Consequently, pike lures should be fished deep. In addition, they should be retrieved as slowly as their action will permit. Indeed, to my mind, the 'hall-mark' of a good pike lure is its ability to combine liveliness with slowness to retrieve. All too often a lure fails to 'work' actively unless it is drawn *rapidly* through the water. While salmon, trout – and, indeed, the majority of predatory fishes – are not averse to chasing a swiftly moving lure, the pike is not of this calibre. A lure passing slowly and seductively past his very nose is much more likely to lure Esox from his underwater lair.

Opinions differ regarding the manner in which the spinning lure should be retrieved. Some experienced anglers maintain that a steady rate of line-recovery produces most results. With this view I find myself in definite disagreement. Admittedly, the steady, even retrieve has accounted for numerous pike, but it is my belief that an irregularly worked lure is much more attractive to pike. Particularly have I found this to be the case where spoon baits are the lures employed. In my favourite spoon technique, a light, lively spoon is cast out and allowed to flutter as it settles in the water. A quick movement of the rod tip brings the lure darting towards the surface after which it is again given time to sink with an attractive side-to-side wobble. This 'tumbling spoon' (Figure 49) technique has often brought me results from waters where other anglers, immediately preceding me and employing a straight, steady retrieve, have failed to 'run' a fish.

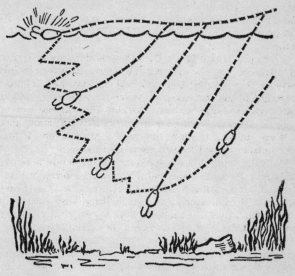

Figure 49 Tumbling spoon

The technique of irregular retrieve need not be confined to spoon baits. Wagtails are rendered more attractive by movements of the rod tip from side to side as the line is recovered. Used thus, the wagtail pursues a zig-zag course with, to my mind, an increased appeal to pike. So, too, with plugs – particularly those of the floating type. Here again the angler can impart added liveliness to his lure by varying the speed of retrieve. The plug should be made to follow an undulating path (Figure 50) by twitching of the rod tip. A plug worked in this fashion constantly changes its depth while, at the same time, varying its rate of wiggle.

Contrary to the dictum of some ancient angling writers, I am wholly against attempts at violent and repeated striking when a pike seizes a spinning lure. Indeed, with modern light tackle such a procedure is definitely impracticable. Effective hooking can be accomplished by an increased tension on the line when the fish is first felt. In its initial lunge the pike will usually hook itself, provided that the hooks are of requisite sharpness. Thereafter continuous – but not necessarily forceful – pressure will do much to maintain contact. In playing a fish, it is advisable to keep the rod tip low. By so doing, strain

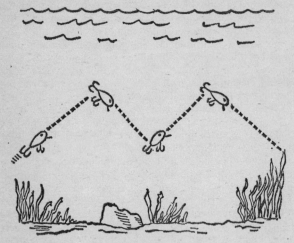

Figure 50 Undulating plug

is imparted *sideways* on the fish, making it more amenable to control in the direction of its 'runs'.

The tactics recommended for river spinning for pike are also largely applicable to spinning for Esox in lakes and similar open waters. Needless to say, there will be some variations in technique, dependent on the different nature of the water.

In this connexion it may be emphasized that on the majority of lakes a boat is almost an essential to successful angling. The best pike grounds in lakes are usually situated on the outer edges of reed beds flanking the shore or in similar places inaccessible to the shore angler. Here and there, perhaps, the angler operating from *terra firma* can cover likely water. Deep, rocky shores, boathouses' jetties, etc, provide opportunities of this nature. In the main, however, shallow verges and areas of intervening vegetation will prevent the exploitation of the most promising prospects. And in spinning for lake pike the angler who covers the greatest area of likely water stands the best chance of covering the most fish. Lake pike tend to be more widespread than their river relatives. Probable pike 'lies' are not so obvious in lakes since, in the absence of strong currents, pike can lurk in any place they choose. With the aid of a boat and a competent boatman the lake angler can cover a surprising extent of water and virtually no territory is inaccessible to his efforts.

In spinning from a boat on large lakes the angler should first decide on the shore which offers the best prospects. Normally, reed-fringed shores, indented with minor bays, hold promise of pike and situations such as those mentioned in the chapter on pike habitat should not be overlooked. If there is a breeze which is directed *towards* the selected shore the boatman should be instructed to row the boat slowly across the wind and along that shore at average casting distance from the shore-line – or, if reeds are present, from the outer edge of the reed beds. The boat's course should run parallel to the contours of the shore-line or the reed beds. There should be no 'short-cutting' across the mouths of bays, etc, since it is in the near-vicinity of the reeds, etc, that pike will most likely be located. Where the breeze is blowing *along* the selected shore, the boat may be allowed to drift with the wind, with such alterations of course as will cause it to follow the natural contours. In this latter case (ie, drifting along the shore), the boat may be taken closer inshore since casting will be mainly directed parallel to – rather than towards – the shore-line. This last-mentioned method is usually the more productive. The angler's lure is searching the water within easy distance of the weeds for almost its entire course and is thus more likely to attract fish.

In actual fishing, the lake angler should not hesitate to vary his tactics. While low-level spinning will normally produce best results, the lure should occasionally be retrieved nearer to the surface. Particularly is this the case for those casts which practically skirt the reed beds. Esox, lurking within the cover of the fringing reed-stems, frequently lies high in the water, on watch for surface-shoaling small fry. Pike, indulging in such tactics, frequently advertise their presence to the angler by splashing or swirling in the shallower bays. Such obvious indications of feeding pike should not be overlooked. The disturbed area and its near-vicinity should be searched *thoroughly* with the lure moving at various depths before hope is abandoned. Lake pike can be too widespread to lightly pass over territory which gives positive evidence of hungry pike.

In the main, however, lake pike lie deep and the angler's lure should be fished accordingly. After casting, the lure should be permitted to sink to a considerable depth before line-recovery is commenced. And it should be remembered that, unless the lure is one incorporating a diving-vane, a steady retrieve results in the lure moving gradually towards the surface. Consequently, if it is desired to fish the lure deep for the major part of its journey, frequent pauses in line-recovery will be necessary to permit the lure to sink in between periods of upward progress.

Operating from a boat, the lake angler will normally be fishing from *open* water towards the pike's lurking places. As a result, when he has hooked a fish, he will seldom have to cope with the difficulties which frequently confront the river angler. Nevertheless, should a heavy pike be hooked, it is advisable to have the boat rowed *slowly* away from nearby reeds during the playing of the fish. Not alone does increased distance from the reeds lessen the chances of disaster from entanglement but it also tends to make the fish fight deeper and closer to the boat with less likelihood of insecure hook-holds giving way.

LIVE BAITING

Angling with live bait is a branch of sport which has been popular with pike anglers for many generations. With one all-important exception, live baiting as practised in modern times follows much the same pattern as it did in the days of our angling forefathers. The vital distinction between modern and ancient live baiting lies in the now almost-extinct practice of gorge fishing, whereby the hapless pike was permitted – indeed, encouraged – to literally 'stomach' the bait and hooks so that escape was well-nigh impossible. Such a practice is, needless to remark, outside the bounds of sporting – and, in many cases, legal – angling, demanding as it does the slaughter of *all* pike landed, irrespective of their size or any other consideration.

Modern live baiting – whereby the bait is presented on

snap-tackle – removes the objections attendant upon gorge fishing. It is mainly an extension of a technique introduced

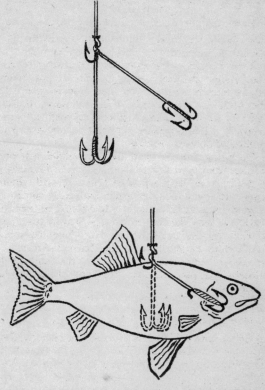

Figure 51 Bickerdyke snap-tackle. Mounted and unmounted. Dotted lines show position of hanging triangle hook on offside of fish

towards the end of the last century and it says much for the genius of the late Mr Alfred Jardine and the late 'John Bickerdyke' that their inventions of that period in the matter of snap-tackle are still commonly employed (Figure 51).

Broadly speaking – live baiting technique may be divided into two categories – viz float fishing and bottom fishing. Each method has its own particular advantages and the wise pike angler will see to it that he is prepared to use either method as conditions indicate.

In this connexion it may be mentioned at the outset that the main items of equipment will serve both purposes. Rod, reel and line remain the same for both methods and only in the matter of terminal tackle are changes necessary. Equipment for live baiting need be in no way elaborate and it is, perhaps,

Figure 52 Live bait mounted on Jardine snap-tackle

this factor more than any other which accounts for the un-doubted popularity of live-bait fishing for pike. Few anglers will aspire to really expensive rods when cheaper ones will satisfy most needs. For those to whom expense is no object it may be mentioned that first-class built-cane rods have all that the most enthusiastic live-bait angler could require. Fibre-glass rods, both hollow and solid, are cheaper and quite effective.

For casting purposes the rod for live baiting should not err on the short side but neither should it be so long as to be unwieldy. Eleven to twelve feet is a fair compromise between efficiency and comfort – and if the rod has a *long* cork handle with adjustable reel fittings so that the reel may be fixed high up on the handle, so much the better. Live baiting demands a stiffish action in the rod both for the purpose of casting weighty baits and for pulling home the hooks in a taking pike. None the less, heavy, unyielding rods should be shunned like the plague. All too often, rods are labelled 'pike-action' when it would need a fish of double figures or more to produce anything approaching sporting action from their barge-pole-like construction. The main feature to avoid is 'whippiness' but it should be remembered that the requisite live baiting 'steeliness' need not be achieved at the sacrifice of moderate weight. The rings on the live bait rod should be large and designed for easy casting. Reference to this feature has been made in the section on spinning rods, but, in passing, it may be well to mention that porcelain-lined rings are commonly used on live bait rods.

Reels for live baiting are obtainable in various models. In the utility class, a free-running 4-inch wooden Nottingham reel with an optional check will not require much outlay but will perform capably. More elaborate – and more costly – centre-pin reels are produced by the various manufacturers in various shapes and sizes. The majority of these are first-class instruments and prove excellent investments for those who can afford them. Not alone are the various additions such as brake-regulators, tension drags, etc, of assistance to the beginner, but in the hands of the expert they can add considerably to the pleasures of angling. Moreover, it should be borne in mind that even the most ardent live-baiter may on occasions be tempted to try his hand at spinning. While spinning of sorts may be accomplished with the cheaper models of centre-pin reels, there is no denying that the specially designed gadgets of the more expensive article enable it to perform much more satisfactorily.

In the matter of lines for live baiting modern invention in the shape of nylon has produced a serious rival to the more old-fashioned silk lines. Unlike the development in fixed spool spinning lines where nylon *monofilament* has gained universal popularity, the line for centre-pin reels should preferably be made of *braided* nylon. This braided nylon line has all the characteristics of the best silk line. In addition, it is rot-proof and dressed lightly with one of the many floatant preparations on the market it is remarkably buoyant. Moreover, although the latest *monofilament* lines are considerably less springy than earlier productions, the braided nylon line has that feeling of 'silkiness' so necessary for trouble-free usage on reels of the centre-pin type.

So much for rod, reel and line for live bait fishing generally. Other items of tackle will vary with the angling method

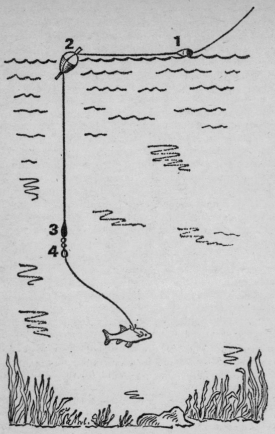

Figure 53 1. Pilot float. 2. Main float. 3. Sinker.
4. Spring link swivel

pursued and will be treated under separate headings. Broadly
speaking live baiting may be divided into two categories: float
fishing and bottom fishing, and prevailing conditions will
normally dictate the method most suitable for employment.

Float fishing is the customary method when underwater
weed growth is extensive and where the current is not over-
strong. A gently moving current or a slight breeze is, if anything, an advantage in float fishing, since the float and live

bait are thereby caused to *rove slowly* through the selected area. Searching the water in this fashion considerably increases the chance of literally laying the lure on Esox's broad and threatening nose. In principle the gear for float fishing consists of float (or floats); lead; and snap-tackle. The reel line should be thoroughly rubbed down with a floatant preparation to pre-

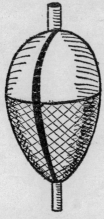

Figure 54 'Fishing Gazette' float

vent it sinking. When fishing in comparatively shallow water with a fixed main float, one (or more) small pilot floats may be attached to the line above the main float to give increased buoyancy (Figure 53).

Various types of floats are available for live baiting. Whatever the model chosen, it should be large enough to resist the bait's efforts to submerge it while at the same time it should not be so bulky as to be insensitive to, or alarmingly resistant to the investigations of a not-so-hungry pike. For shallow-water fishing where the float can be firmly fixed to the reel line, the *Fishing Gazette* type (Figure 54) is probably the most satisfactory. In this model, the line is inserted into the float through a slit in the side, where it is kept in place by means of a removable peg. This feature ensures that a change of fishing depth entails but the work of a few seconds – a commendable asset in a sport where experiment frequently pays high dividends.

In deep water it will frequently be found that the depth at which it is desired to suspend the bait below the float is greater than the length of the rod. In such circumstances, it is necessary to use a 'slider' type of float (Figure 55). The sliding float is so constructed that as the line is wound in previous to casting the float slides down the line until it is halted by the

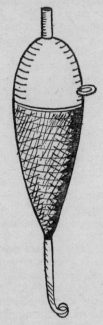

Figure 55 Sliding float

lead. When the cast is completed and the bait sinks in the water, the buoyancy of the sliding float causes it to slide back up the line until its upward progress is arrested by a small rubber stop, previously hitched into the line at the required depth.

Below the float and at a distance of several feet from the terminal tackle, the lead (or sinker) should be attached to the line. This lead may be of several shapes. The elongated Jardine spiral lead is an excellent pattern but pierced leads with the line running down the centre – either spherical or barrel-shape – are alternative and useful forms of sinkers.

The connexion between the lead and the snap-tackle is usually effected by means of a trace. Many experienced live-baiters omit the trace altogether and extend the reel line below the lead to join direct to the snap-tackle. For those who prefer a trace – and I am one of them – choice may be made between a strand of non-rusting trace wire and a length of monofilament nylon. Personally, I prefer the nylon trace on the grounds that it is inconspicuous; impervious to kinking; and tough enough to resist the onslaughts of the teeth of most pike. At the lower end of the trace (or the line, if a trace be dispensed with), a spring-link swivel should be attached as a quick and easy means of joining on the snap-tackle.

The snap-tackle – ie, the hook flight on which the live bait is mounted – can be of various forms. For general usefulness, however, the patterns known respectively as the 'Jardine' (Figure 52) and the 'Bickerdyke' (Figure 51) are deservedly popular among pike anglers. Reference to the illustrations will, I think, more clearly indicate their main features than will attempts at written description. Of the two designs, the 'Bickerdyke' is probably the more effective – embodying, as it does, a treble-hook on *each* side of the bait. Nevertheless, it cannot be overlooked that the 'Jardine' snap-tackle is used to the exclusion of all others by many experienced live-baiters.

A more simple form of snap-tackle consists merely of a dorsal single hook from which a treble hook is suspended so that it hangs level with the lower edge of the bait. Such an arrangement certainly makes for a lively bait, requiring, as it does, but one small piercing at the root of the dorsal fin. Its hooking qualities are also reasonably satisfactory, but its main fault lies in the insecurity of attachment to the bait. For long-range casting it is definitely inferior to the patterns mentioned earlier.

Still simpler is a single hook through the upper jaw of a small live bait. (See 'Minnow Fishing' for Perch.)

Turning from tackle to tactics, the first matter of import-ance is the depth at which to fish. In the main this will depend largely on prevailing conditions. In clear, shallow water, for example, the bait should swim at mid-water or even higher. When the water is coloured and visibility conse-quently much reduced, the float should be set so that the live bait works a matter of a foot or so over the weeds on the bottom. In water deep enough to require the use of a slider float, the lower levels of the water are usually more productive of pike and the float should be adjusted accordingly. It must be emphasized, however, that – as in all matters piscatorial – no set rules can be laid down to suit all circumstances. The experienced angler, therefore, will not hesitate to alter fishing depth if the indicated level fails to produce results.

A primary consideration of the live-baiter will be the keeping of his baits in best condition. Of first importance in this connexion is a container for the baits. This should, if possible, be of ample size and fitted with an inner removable receptacle of perforated material to permit of easy access to the baits and also to assist in aeration of the water. It is not only in the bait-can, however, that care should be taken with the baits. It cannot be over-emphasized that a lively bait is much more likely to attract pike than is a half-dead bait. Consequently, care must be exercised in the attachment of the live bait to the snap-tackle. The bait should be held securely – *but not tightly* – when affixing the hooks and these should not be inserted any deeper than is absolutely necessary. The operation is made considerably easier if the hooks are honed to needle-sharpness.

In actual angling tactics, too, the welfare of the bait is a major consideration. Unnecessarily long and strenuous casts should be avoided and, in all casts, the bait should be swung – pendulum-fashion – rather than forcibly cast, to the selected spot. Retrieving the bait should be done slowly, and the bait should not be kept out of the water for longer than is necessary. It is here that the link-spring swivel at the bottom of the trace shows its worth. When changing this scene of operations, the angler can easily unclip his armed bait from the trace and thus give his lure a longer lease of life by carrying it in the bait-can.

In actual angling procedure, the live-baiter may choose either of two courses. He may play a waiting game somewhat after the manner of the pike itself. This he does by choosing what he believes to be productive water and there setting his baited tackle in the hope that, sooner or later, Esox will arrive to sample his offering. Alternatively, he may make his sport a semi-active one by casting his live bait into, first, one likely haunt and then, if results are not quickly forthcoming, soon moving on to another scene of operations. Personally, I prefer a compromise – dallying where the water looks particularly

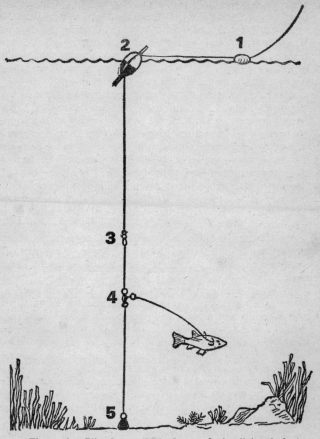

Figure 56 1. Pilot float. 2. Main float. 3. Spring-link swivel.
4. Three-way swivel and paternoster. 5. Sinker

promising but never hesitating to move to new ground when
hope starts to dwindle.

Concerning bottom fishing with live bait, it should be noted
that much of the matter discussed in the pages on float fishing
will also be applicable to angling either with paternoster or
with ledger.

The paternoster may be used under most pike angling

conditions except when underwater weed is thick and widespread. It is particularly effective where strong currents
predominate and where float-tackle is likely to be swept
downstream too rapidly. As a means of fishing clearings in
heavy underwater cover, too, the paternoster excels and it is
decidedly useful for searching likely pike haunts at some considerable distance from the angler.

Fundamentally the paternoster consists of a trace termin-
ating in a suitable sinker and to which the live bait is attached

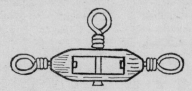

Figure 57 Three-way paternoster swivel

at a predetermined distance from the bottom. Opinions vary
as to the relative merits of the boom or the plain paternoster.
In the former, the baited snap-tackle is attached to a short
wire (or plastic) boom fixed at right angles to the trace. The
underlying principle is that a bait thus attached is less liable to
tangle round the trace. My own preference is for a plain
paternoster – a straightforward arrangement, in which the
junction of snap-tackle with trace is effected by means of a
three-way swivel (Figure 57).

To minimize the possible danger of tangles, the paternoster
trace should hang in the water in as near as possible to a
vertical position. When angling close to bank (or boat) this is a
simple matter since the line will hang almost straight down
from the rod tip. Angling farther afield is a more complex
matter and a compromise between float and paternoster tackle
is indicated. As will be obvious, a paternoster used without a
float and cast some considerable distance from the angler will
make an acute angle with the bottom. Not only will this affect
the distance from the bottom at which the bait is fished but it
also leads to tangled gear. A small float, lacking sufficiency to
lift the sinker clear of the bottom, will, nevertheless, help to
hold the trace vertical, thus removing the disadvantages attendant on a deeply slanting gear. The distance of the snap-
tackle from the lead will – if the trace is vertical – govern the
depth at which the live bait swims. Generally speaking, 12 to

184

18 ins from the bottom is a likely depth unless weeds are prevalent, in which case the same distance above the *tops* of the weeds is recommended. Here again, however, as in float fishing, trial and error is an able ally, for what may suit on one occasion may prove ineffective on another.

SNAP-TROLLING AND TRAILING

Trolling with snap-tackle is a mode of pike angling which somehow is not so popular as it might be. Like modern live baiting with snap-tackle, snap-trolling is a sporting adaptation of the ancient method of fishing known as gorge-baiting. Thus, it is possible that the stigma of gorge fishing is responsible for the lack of popularity attached to snap-trolling. If this is so, many pike anglers are labouring under a delusion, for modern snap-trolling is definitely a sporting method of angling. Moreover, it is an extremely effective one, particularly in very weedy water where other methods of angling are at a discount. If snap-trolling should need further recommendation it is to be found in the fact that, being something of a compromise between spinning and live baiting, snap-trolling provides the angler possessing a modest outfit with an active sport entailing as much exercise as he may desire.

Basically, snap-trolling consists of dropping an armed dead bait into the pike haunts so that it darts head downwards, in seductive manner towards the bottom. The requisite tackle is simple, being nothing more than a long narrow body-lead to which is attached hook tackle. The accompanying diagram illustrates an effective type of snap-trolling tackle, but minor alterations may be made to suit individual requirements (Figure 58).

Before describing the technique of snap-trolling it may be advisable to differentiate between the methods of pike angling known respectively as 'trolling' and 'trailing'. The term *'trolling'* – as originally and correctly used – refers *only* to the method wherein the angler, remaining stationary, works his bait on a 'sink-and-draw' principle in a vertical direction in the water. Unfortunately, the descriptive term *'trolling'* has, of latter years, become linked with that form of fishing, properly called *'trailing'*, wherein a lure is trailed behind a moving boat – the lures, as it were, being left to fish by themselves. As a result, it is not uncommon to hear of large pike (especially

lake pike) having been taken by 'trolling' when in actual fact
the fish were caught by trailing and neither tackle nor method
had the remotest relationship with the term 'troll', as correctly
used.

Reverting to the technique of snap-trolling, it may be mentioned that a long rod is a definite asset since the main object
is to drop – rather than cast – the bait into the pike haunts.

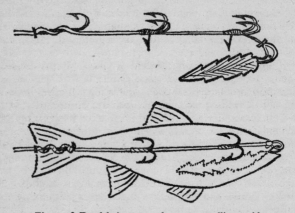

Figure 58 Dead-bait mounted on snap-trolling tackle

The body-lead should be heavy enough to cause the bait to
dive, head foremost, at moderate speed towards the bottom.
No attempt should be made to impart a curve to the bait on
the tackle.

The bait should be dropped into open spaces in the weeds
or into deep holes which advertise themselves as likely pike
haunts. As the dropped bait is about to enter the water, the
rod tip should be lowered and sufficient slack line let run until
the bait reaches close to the bottom. If the initial dive fails to
produce results, the rod tip should be raised smartly to lift the
bait a yard or so in the water, after which the rod should be
again lowered quickly to allow the bait to glide once more
rapidly downwards. This 'sink-and-draw' process need not be
repeated for long in the one place. If a hungry pike is about
and sees the bait, he will likely effect an early contact. After
half a dozen or so dives without result, the angler should
move on to the next likely holding-place where Fate may be
more kind. In this fashion, a considerable amount of water

may be covered in an outing and it is odds-on that in the journey the snap-troll will connect with foraging pike.

More often than not a pike seizing a trolled bait does so as the bait is on its downward course. The resulting bite will usually not be felt by the angler until he lifts the rod tip on the next draw. Any feeling of resistance should be answered by an instant tightening of the line, for delay will likely result in what is virtually a reversion to 'gorge' methods. Any form of strong reel will prove suitable for snap-trolling since casting is at a discount, and the line used should be strong (at least 10 lb breaking strain) since much of the fishing will take place in heavily weeded water.

Trailing as a sporting method of pike fishing is decried by many anglers. Yet, on lakes and similar large waters there are few more productive methods. And while trailing is in no way an artistic angling method, it at least has the merit of enabling the angler to connect with pike – and often heavy fish at that. Provided that the tackle used is not over-heavy, such fish can provide ample excitement so that, by and large, it would seem that the indictments frequently levelled against trailing are not entirely justified.

Suitable tackle for sporting trailing consists of the bait-casting outfit described earlier under the heading of spinning tackle. Admittedly, much heavier gear is frequently employed but such extra strength and stiffness is by no means necessary and, indeed, is mainly responsible for the ill-repute which surrounds the sport of trailing. With the short bait-casting rod and the multiplier reel, a hooked pike requires skill in playing and, if the fish should be a 'big 'un', the angler will likely enjoy considerable sport before the fish is either captured or lost.

Either dead baits or artificial lures may be used for trailing. If natural bait is preferred, the fish selected should, if possible, be a slim-bodied species, since this shape spins better and puts less strain on the tackle than does a deep-bodied bait. In this connexion, a small fresh herring makes an admirable bait for trailing and its silvery flash holds much attraction for foraging pike. The dead bait should be mounted on tackle similar to that used in spinning with dead bait, but, to prevent kinking of the line, it is essential that *free-working* swivels and an anti-kink device of some sort are incorporated in the trace.

Artificial lures for trailing may be any of those used normally for spinning. For preference, however, the lure for trailing should be both larger and heavier than the average spinning lure. A large lively spoon is excellent, but heavy spoons frquently lack action when drawn slowly through the water. Wagtails are also first-rate trailing lures, especially in 4-in size and upwards. Best of all lures for trailing, however, is probably the large, jointed plug. Such a lure exhibits no tendency to kink the line, and it has the further advantage that it can be made to run at varying depths simply by rowing slower or faster as the occasion demands.

In trailing, the boat should be rowed slowly and the lure should be trailed *at least* 30 yds behind the boat. A course parallel to and close in to the edges of the weed beds is usually the most productive – and when a pike takes, the hooks should be pulled home sharply to overcome any slackness in the long length of trailing line. Line should be shortened as quickly as possible so that the fish may be got under angling control. Efficient manoeuvring of the boat can assist greatly in this respect, but a slack line must be avoided at all costs if the hook-hold is to remain secure.

Dead baits are being used with increasing success on ledger tackle for taking pike. The normal snap-tackle is useful but since you are dealing with a dead fish an arrangement of one hook near the tail and one coming out of the gills is equally effective.

Small freshwater fish are useful as baits but herrings and large sprats have proved even more successful.

KENNETH MANSFIELD

? Perch (*Perca fluviatilus*)
(*For description, see Appendix I*)

SPAWNING AND GROWTH

Perch, already gregarious, have no need to gather together for
the purpose of mating as do some more solitary fish – though
they may be joined by a few large and normally solitary specimens – and as spawning time approaches they move to still or
slowly moving water where the bottom is for preference a
sand or gravel one containing reeds or other plants, branches
of trees or numerous stones. Here the female lays her eggs.
The eggs exude from the female perch embedded in a ribbon
of jelly-like membrane, the end of which the fish affixes to or
entangles in some convenient underwater fixed point such as a
reed stem, a sunken branch or a stone. Then, as the female
moves forward in a series of jerks, the ribbon of eggs is drawn
from her body and the male exudes his milt over them.
Counts showing that a perch weighing $\frac{1}{2}$ lb laid 250,000 eggs,
and one weighing 1 lb laid only a few thousand short of a
million. Such prodigality is necessary, since the eggs suffer
more severe depredations from the creatures of water and
land than do the eggs of other species, for the floating ribbons
of jelly are clearly visible, and fish and birds take heavy toll of
them. Frequently some portion of the egg ribbon adheres to
the feet of a migrant water bird, and when the bird moves on
to another water it may take the eggs with it and deposit them
in a fishless pond where the subsequent appearance of perch
causes a minor mystery.

In from fourteen to twenty-two days, according to the temperature of the water, the alevins hatch, their length at hatch-
ing being about 5 mm. These sink to the bottom, where they
remain for about a month until the yolk-sac is absorbed. They
then rise to the surface waters and live as fry upon planktonic
animal matter. For two years their growth is rapid, but their
subsequent growth depends upon the amount of food

available in the water. Professor Gunmer Alm, Director of the Swedish State Institute of Freshwater Fishing Research, has studied perch over a number of years. He found that nearly all perch grew at approximately the same rate for two years, but with some perch growth virtually stopped at that age; some grew very slowly; and some shot ahead to become really big perch: but the differences only occurred in different waters, and all the perch in any one particular water grew to approximately the same maximum size. Lake A might contain numbers of 2-lb perch, but there would be very few over that weight and the only ones under it would be growing fish that might be expected eventually to reach 2 lb. Lake B, though the same size as Lake A, might produce perch with a maximum size of only 2 oz. In these circumstances there would be far more perch in Lake B than in Lake A, and the apparent reason for the low maximum size of the smaller fish is food supply, for many experiments have proved that if perch in overcrowded waters are thinned out, the maximum size of the remainder increases. That this may take a long time is shown by experiments undertaken at Lake Windermere. Windermere perch averaged about 1 oz in weight and were numbered in millions. In order to reduce their numbers they were regularly trapped, and between 1941 and 1954 well over 100 tons were removed without effect on the average size of the perch. Gradually the lower demands on food began to tell, and by 1958 increases of up to 800 per cent were recorded.

Generally speaking, perch sizes are dependent on food supply. Where this is insufficient the fish are undersized, and waters which teem with these small fish are best avoided by anglers, for there is little hope of catching large specimens; and pulling out 2-oz perch every minute or so becomes monotonous if not exasperating. An angler who knows of such a water and is a member of the club that owns the fishing rights should do his utmost to induce the committee to remove about 75 per cent of the perch in order that the remainder may have a chance of growing larger and begetting offspring worth catching, or, better still, remove them all and replace them with known good stock.

GENERAL

Perch are gregarious fish that move around in shoals seeking their food with considerable activity, but the angler faced with the problem of where to find perch should bear in mind the fact that though they are wanderers, each shoal remains within self-prescribed limits unless driven elsewhere by outside influences such as pollution or a sudden failure in the food supply. In small ponds and in short stretches of canal between locks, the angler can fish from any convenient position, confident in the knowledge that if perch are feeding at all they will eventually come upon his bait in their wanderings. In the larger lakes, in rivers, and in canals not partially sealed by frequent locks, there are likely to be many large areas of water into which perch never roam, and it is obviously a waste of time to fish for them in these.

My study of perch in canals has led me to the belief that many shoals of perch follow definite routes in their search for food, and that, unless suddenly disturbed, the fish keep to these tracks. They will first, perhaps, follow one bank, and then, for a reason known only to themselves, cross to the other, repeating this change of course every time that particular shoal passes that way. Knowledge such as this is invaluable to an angler, and he is likely to do well if he can trace the course of a group of big perch. What is true of canal perch is probably true of lake perch. They are difficult to see and track in lakes but if their route can be seen or inferred it solves the main problem of summer fishing in big lakes for perch – that of finding the fish.

Fortunately perch have a marked liking for certain natural and artificial features, particularly those on which weed is likely to grow; partially because they themselves like nosing into weed for what animal food it may contain, but mainly because small fry, also weed loving, may assemble in the area and provide meals for perch. Among the objects and situations which attract perch are the brickwork or ironwork of bridges; any woodwork which lines the bank or juts into the water; derelict barges; wharves, quays, steps, etc; outcrops of rock; roots of trees; and sunken inlet or outlet pipes. Apart from the food-finding possibilities of these positions, already noted, they provide cover for very big perch from which they can dash out on their prey.

It is difficult to lay down a dividing line between big and very big perch, but when I write of big perch I am thinking of fish from about 1½ to 2 lb in weight that still move in shoals – though possibly shoals of only three or four fish. Very big perch – 3 lb and upwards – are often solitary, possibly the sole survivors of their hatch, and they develop the pike-like habit of lying in wait for their food instead of actively chasing it. This is important, for they are unlikely to be caught with stationary baits. The wandering angler with float or paternoster and the angler spinning a lure are most likely to encounter them. In winter they are sometimes found on the move, and there is evidence that in the deeper bodies of water (ie, in deep lakes and reservoirs) even these very big and normally solitary perch tend to congregate at the bottom in the deepest parts.

With these points in mind it will now be possible to consider their application to six general types of waters – rivers; canals; ponds and small lakes; big lakes; reservoirs; and gravel pits.

RIVERS

Only exceptionally are perch found in swift shallow rivers. They are sometimes present in rivers where long deep pools alternate with riffles, but their preference is for comparatively deep slow-flowing rivers and streams.

In *summer* they like to lie in deep holes, preferably near the banks, but on their foraging expeditions they often cruise in surface waters, the larger of them causing fry to leap in frightened shoals from the water. Very big perch, when feeding, are likely to lie up in weed patches. In their travels the roving perch are likely to visit any of the places mentioned earlier as typical perch haunts, and on really hot days they have a preference for shade, so the shaded side of some rock or structure is a position which may well harbour them. Deep holes among the roots of a tree whose shadow falls on the water is another excellent position. In backwaters and on stretches of the river where the current is really slow, weeds and rushes will be plentiful, and it is profitable to fish along the edges of these, and especially along beds of water-lilies and in gaps between them.

In *autumn* their situation is likely to be the same as in summer, but if the river has many trees and bushes on its banks there will be accumulations of leaves at certain places on the river bed, not necessarily under the trees themselves. In rivers with an irregular bed the leaves generally accumulate at the head of every deep pool where the current starts to slacken with the greater depth. Perch (and most other fish) avoid these places on account of gases given off by the decomposing leaves, and anglers should follow their example – though I must add that perch seem to be less fussy in this respect than several other species.

In *winter* the places favoured by perch in a river depend to a great extent on the level of the water. Normally this is considerably higher than the average summer flow and it may from time to time assume flood proportions as prolonged rain or melting snow swells the volume of water. Abnormally it may be very little higher than in summer.

As a generalization (which has its exceptions) all fish seek deeper water in winter, and the colder the surface water, the farther away from it they like to get. Perch are carnivorous fish and once they have attained a few inches of length they become largely predatory. In addition to the natural inclination to seek deeper water, they will be found deep down because it is there that their prey will be found; and this applies particularly to the bigger specimens.

Subject to these factors, which are governed by water temperature, perch will still be found in the type of haunt they delight in – the weed-forming surfaces mentioned earlier in this section. The angler will, therefore, expect to find perch in the deep pools by bridge supports; in deep water alongside quays; in long, deep, quiet pools; and in eddies where the current reverses its direction and scours out a hole.

Under floodwater conditions perch may be found anywhere out of the force of the main current. They dislike intensely a battle against swift water, and as a spate rises they will move into drainage ditches and small tributary streams when these are available. If there are none, the perch may be found in comparatively sheltered water behind any obstruction to the main stream, whether it be a rock, a jetty, a bridge support or a fallen tree. Eddies, more numerous and covering a larger area in flood than in normal conditions, are particularly good places for perch at such a time.

CANALS

Canal perch lead a placid life undisturbed by more than an occasional hunting pike and by the baits and lures of anglers. There is usually ample food, especially in the many canals no longer used by traffic, for weed grows luxuriantly and supports a very heavy stock of the insects, molluscs and crustaceans which form a proportion of a perch's food. The same creatures, and the plants themselves, feed large shoals of fry of other species of fish which play their part in feeding perch.

Canals are usually of uniform depth, and the difference between summer, autumn and winter levels is likely to be slight except in drought, when some canals suffer badly. Deeper water is often found between the bricks or stone approaches to locks and in the locks themselves, and in addition to all the previously mentioned haunts that are applicable to canals, these places are well worth a trial. This is especially true in very hot or very cold weather, though neither condition is a good one for perch fishing in waters less than 10 ft deep. Positions under trees, which may be excellent in summer, are best avoided when the leaves are falling and for a week or two after that time.

By using towpaths it is generally possible to cover considerable distances along canals interrupted by only negligible obstacles, and for this reason they are peculiarly fitted to the roving perch angler, whose fishing is described in detail in the section on fishing methods.

PONDS AND SMALL LAKES

The quality of perch fishing anywhere depends almost entirely upon the quantity of food available in the water, and this factor is of the greatest importance in ponds or small lakes. In rivers, canals and large lakes perch have room to move, and if food is short in one area they will move to another. In the waters under discussion they have to make do with whatever food is available. If this is inadequate, and the perch breed, generation will follow generation, the perch increasing in number and decreasing in size until the water swarms with mature but tiny perch. There are far too many of these ponds, and they have given perch fishing a bad name as a whole. It is quite hopeless to fish them, for though one or two of the older stock may have waxed fat on their stunted kindred, it is almost impossible to fish for them except with live bait too big for attack by the smaller fish.

Fortunately there are hundreds of small lakes and ponds – including mill ponds – where the food is plentiful and in which perch grow to a good sporting size. If a boat is available on such waters I like to use it, for in addition to allowing one to cover areas not in reach from the bank, it enables one to fish the outer edges of reed banks which, though close to the shore, are often unfishable from it. The boat should be anchored at full casting distance from the fishing spot in order to disturb the fish as little as possible.

When one has to fish from the bank it is advisable to choose some obvious perch haunt such as an outcrop of rock or a jetty, but if, as is usually the case, there is no such outstanding feature it is perhaps best to take up a position from which one can cast into water just beyond the shore shallows.

When perch are feeding they move round and round their enclosed waters seeking whatever is to be found, and they should eventually come upon the stationary angler's bait.

BIG LAKES

Big lakes are the most difficult of all waters for perch fishing, for it seems that in most of them there are considerable areas into which perch never come. Each school of perch seems to have its limited range, and providing that food supplies are maintained they do not leave it until late autumn or early winter, when they congregate before taking up their deep-water winter quarters. The matter is further complicated in deep lakes by the depth at which the perch are feeding. They do not like sudden changes of depth, and considerable study of many factors – which differ with different lakes – is necessary before the right depth can be found by deduction. The alternative is trial and error, but this method is not recommended to those spending only a brief fishing holiday on a big lake.

The visitor's best plan is to seek advice from resident anglers. Through long years of experience they may know the best perch haunts and may be willing to give some idea of the best places and depths at which to fish in prevailing conditions.

The main factor governing the position of perch is water temperature. In summer the very big perch are difficult to find, for they may be solitary, and in the acres of weed that afford them cover for their attacks upon their prey they may be anywhere, subject to temperature. They are unlikely to be in the depths, for the water there is relatively cold and possibly lacking in oxygen, so that very few of the fish on which perch feed would be found there. They will favour the places favoured by shoals of small fish, and, since the latter can be fairly easily observed, they offer a possible guide to big perch.

When there is no wind the water is in roughly horizontal temperature layers, with the warmer water at the surface; and fishing should be confined to the upper layers. When a wind is blowing, currents alter the position of the water layers. The water is likely to be cold on the side from which the wind is blowing and warm on the side to which the wind is blowing. On the 'warm' side, the relatively warm water goes much deeper than on a windless day, and it is profitable to fish on that side at a greater depth.

In cold winter weather the water at the bottom is likely to be warmer than that at the surface, and perch should be sought in the deepest areas.

RESERVOIRS

Little can be said about reservoir fishing for perch except that each reservoir has its peculiarities and that perch are not generally easy to catch. Anglers must be prepared to find the best positions, baits and depths for themselves, and this demands a good deal more than a casual day's fishing. The water is often deep and a sliding float will be necessary if a float is used at all. Positions near inlet and outlet pipes are always worth trying.

I feel that some of the bigger reservoirs that include perch among their fish population may well contain some almost unbelievably big specimens. In those reservoirs where live baiting is barred it might be well to try deep-diving plugs, but a really big lobworm on sliding paternoster, ledger or wander tackle, or in conjunction with a shining, hookless spoon as an attractor, is likely to prove killing.

GRAVEL PITS

A great many old gravel pits have filled with water and have been stocked with fish. Some of them hold good perch. They are usually at least 10 ft deep, often straight-sided, and frequently almost devoid of plant growth. There are not, as a rule, many obvious perch haunts, but if derelict rails, tip trucks, wooden ramps, etc, are visible, these are the places to try.

Gravel pits do not normally contain such a wealth of natural food as do ponds, canals and rivers; and in my rather limited experience of this type of water I have found the perch to be more than usually predatory, so that live baiting and spinning will give better results than bait fishing. Unless one knows of clear places, paternostering and ledgering should be avoided, for the bottoms of gravel pits are often full of snags.

Clay pits usually encourage prolific plant growth.

BAITS

The section on baits covers this subject and it is necessary only to say that lobworms and small live baits are the recognized attractors.

BAITING THE HOOK

I have no reason to believe that perch are put off by the sight of a hook. I usually hook worms once through the body below the band. This leaves a good 'wriggling' portion, an essential with a fish which feeds in the main on living creatures.

A baited two-hook Pennell tackle is illustrated in Figure 59.

Figure 59 Baited Pennell tackle

If these are used the strike must be quick, for if a perch should happen to gorge the bait it is almost impossible to free it without killing the fish.

Live baits are best used on single hooks inserted in the gristle of the upper lip (Figure 60).

1 inch

Figure 60

METHODS

Perch may be caught by most of the standard methods described elsewhere in this book. They include float fishing, long-trotting, ledgering in all its forms, paternostering with ordinary or live bait, spinning and free lining. The last two deserve a special mention in relation to perch fishing.

SPINNING

General

Spinning for perch is an energetic and absorbing method of fishing, but until fairly recent years its popularity with anglers has been limited by the mechanics of spinning tackle. The ideal lures for perch spinning are comparatively light and, in days when only revolving drum and multiplying reels were available, the weight of the lure was often insufficient to overcome the inertia of the reel for lengthy casts. The advent of the fixed spool reel has brought about a revolution in spinning for perch.

Lures can be spun or fished directly from the end of the line, but I prefer to have 2 ft of monofilament between the end of the line and the lure. This is secured to the end of the line by a swivel, and to the lure by a link swivel (Figure 61). Even with lures such as plugs, which are not supposed to spin, swivels are desirable, and the link swivel at the end enables one to change the lure in a few seconds.

Lures

Any of the vast array of the smaller spinners, spoons and plugs may catch perch, but I have never caught a perch with a lure longer than 2 ins. With this reservation anything that suits the conditions may be successful. By conditions I mean (to take two extremes) a heavy lure like a metal devon for winter deep-water spinning and a floating plug for a weed-ridden canal in high summer.

Small dead baits mounted on spinning flights can also be killers.

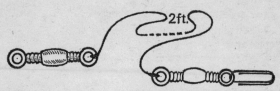

Figure 61 Light spinning trace lures on the link swivel can be changed quickly

Spinning Tactics

Armed with a spinning rod, and the reel, lines and lure of his choice, the angler can commence operations. Spinning can be done from bank or boat in any water that holds perch, and the most successful angler will be he who can decide where perch are to be found, and who can then cast accurately to a spot from which the lure will pass the supposed fish in its line of recovery.

Most anglers agree that a jerky recovery is more likely to attract perch than a straightforward reeling-in. Two or three feet of line are recovered, followed by a pause in reeling which allows the lure to sink a little before it is further recovered. This process is continued until the lure is close to the angler's bank, and alertness should never be relaxed until the lure is out of the water. There is rarely any doubt about a perch's take. The pluck should be followed by an instantaneous and momentary holding of the line, which is sufficient to fix the hooks without a strike, though a little delay rarely loses a fish when *natural* baits are being spun.

Spinning Season

Spinning can be done throughout the open season, but it offers the maximum amount of sport in winter when the weeds have died down. In cold weather the lure should fish deep, and I therefore favour a heavy devon or a deep-diving plug at that time. In summer, lighter lures can be used higher in the water.

I have adapted the 'baited spoon' method of flounder fishing to fishing for winter perch in deep water. I fix a 3-inch hookless spoon, silvered on both sides, to the line some 4 ft from the hook. The hook is baited with a large lobworm. The theory is that the flash of the spoon in the dim depths arouses interest. I have caught nothing heavier than a perch of 1 lb, but the system works. The tackle must be allowed to sink almost to the bottom before slow recovery is begun (Figure 62).

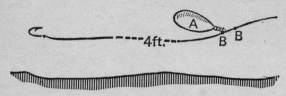

Figure 62 A. Hookless 3-in spoon. B. Split shot stops

WANDER TACKLE

I have taken this name, and the main arrangement of tackle, from another scheme designed for flounder fishing. In the limited experiments I have made with it I have caught perch of a pound and over. The tackle is illustrated in Figure 63.

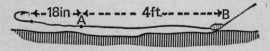

Figure 63 Wander tackle. A. Split shot. B. ¼-oz spiral lead

A ¼-oz spiral lead is fixed to the cast 4 ft from the hook. Eighteen inches from the hook there is a big split shot. This tackle can be used only on a lake or part of a lake with a weed- and snag-free bottom, and these conditions must extend almost to the bank unless a boat is used. The tackle is cast out as far as possible and allowed to sink to the bottom. It is then recovered very slowly. The heavier weight drags along the bottom and stirs up mud or gravel. A sight-hunting fish is likely to be attracted to this, and the following bait may be found.

The conditions are not easy to find, and for that reason I have fished in this way less often than I would have liked. So far I have used only a large lobworm as a bait, but it is possible that a small dead fish might prove successful.

If the bottom is known to be clear and very long casts are desirable, heavier weights can be used.

TROLLING OR 'SINK AND DRAW'

This is another excellent method of fishing for perch on a 'roving commission'. It is particularly useful in summer on well-weeded waters.

The tackle consists of the usual rod (the longest if there is any choice), reel and line. The bait consists of a weighted dead fish, mounted on tackles made for the purpose. These tackles differ a good deal in the number and size of the hooks, and in the shape and weight of the leads, but their principle is the same. The lead is inserted through the mouth of the dead gudgeon, minnow, etc, that is being used as bait, and the hooks are mounted in its flesh.

It will be seen that the head end of the fish, which holds the lead, will enter the water first. At the waterside the bait is merely swung out to the required spot, preferably in a clearing in the weeds. The bait dives head-foremost to the bottom. It is allowed to remain there for a moment and then the rod tip is slowly raised a foot or two. The bait will rise, and at the same time swing in a little towards the angler. If weeds allow it, the bait can be worked in to the angler's bank. If they do not, the bait is raised from its hole and a trial is made elsewhere. Every likely spot should be fished thoroughly, but it is not often necessary to remain for more than three or four minutes in one place.

This is an interesting way of fishing, for it calls for constant action, and the bait is particularly attractive to big perch. The bait is taken in a swift rush, and it is not usually necessary to strike.

This method is correctly known as trolling, a word which is, unfortunately, being used increasingly for fishing by towing a lure or bait behind a moving boat.

FREE LINE FISHING

A pleasant method of fishing any water fairly free of weeds and snags is free-line fishing. Almost any rod and reel will do, though I find the best outfit a 10-or 11-ft rod and a fixed spool reel. The finer the line and cast the better. Neither float nor weight is used. The bait, usually a worm or small live bait, is put on the hook and cast into likely water. Worms sink naturally to the bottom, whence they can be recovered very slowly and cast again. Live bait can be given their heads and allowed to swim where they will. A 3-lb line is heavy enough for fishing in this way. If there is a wind, it is desirable to have it behind or nearly behind one.

NOTE ON PIKE-PERCH

Pike-perch are closely related to perch, but are separate species and not hybrids of pike and perch.

One is the European pike-perch, generally known on the Continent as the zander or sander: and the other is the American pike-perch, known throughout North America as the walleye. Detailed 'specifications' will be found in Appendix I. None of the species is indigenous to the British Isles. The history of American importations is vague, but an 11¾-lb fish caught in the River Delph, Cambridgeshire, as long ago as 1934 was accepted as a walleye record. There have been several importations from the Continent but little was heard about them until the Leighton Buzzard A.C. put stock in some local wet pits. There they flourished and aroused considerable interest. Since then a good deal of stocking has been done in suitable waters in many parts of the country, but fish of a sporting size seem still to be confined to the Bedfordshire-Cambridgeshire area. The record European pike-perch (zander) was caught in the Great Ouse Relief Channel in 1971 (15 lb 5 oz).

There is no doubt that these fish have a brilliant future. They grow to a good size, take readily when in the mood and do not appear to have any really destructive effect upon the stocks of native fish on which they feed.

They will take worm baits, but the standard bait is a live fish, normally fished well down. They have also been taken on artificial lures and on dead fish mounted on spinning flights.

I have no experience of them in English waters, but caught many in German rivers some years ago – always on live bait.

In addition to their sporting attractions they are very good to eat – and in years to come I think we shall hear much more of them.

KENNETH MANSFIELD

The Common Eel (*Anguilla anguilla*)

Every English coarse fishing angler must have caught eels, so
there is no need for detailed description.

A brief note about their life history is necessary. It is a
subject which has been worked to exhaustion in the press and
on radio and television, but these popular expositions usually
take us only to the time when the elver turns into a tiny eel.
The angler who sets out to catch eels is more interested in its
later history.

European eels spawn in great depths in the Caribbean Sea.
The eggs produce tiny willow-leaf-shaped larvae which are

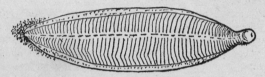

Figure 64 Leptocephalus

carried by the Gulf Stream and its Drifts to the shores of
Europe. The larvae are known as leptocephali. They take approximately three years to cross the Atlantic and in that time
they grow to a length of about 3 ins. When they reach the
brackish water of estuaries they turn into elvers; slim, cylindrical, 3-ins, practically transparent creatures that in a short
time become small but true eels. A leptocephalus that 'puts
into', say, Falmouth turns into an elver weeks before a similar
one of the same hatch does so if its destination is a Scan-
dinavian or Icelandic river. That is a minor mystery. A major
one is that American eels share the spawning ground with
European eels, but, although they take only one and a half to
two years to reach their rivers, they still turn to elvers when
they reach their estuaries.

British elvers ascend the estuaries and are in some places
netted and sold by the million to be made into elver cakes and

other delicacies. Those that escape human, bird, and fish predators, work their way upstream, overcoming what may seem to us impassable obstacles. They quickly become tiny but true eels and continue upstream, large numbers turning off, as inclination takes them, into tributaries, backwaters, ditches and, on wet days, to ponds and lakes which they reach overland through the wet grass. Many continue upstream to the ultimate limit of the waterway. In general, males remain in the lower reaches. By the time full summer has come, new contingents of eels have joined the resident populations in every accessible water in the British Isles.

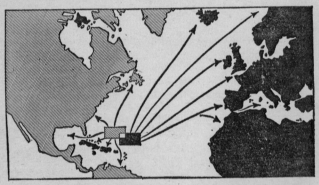

Figure 65 Eels' breeding area. Black rectangle – European eels. Shaded rectangle – North American eels

The incomers remain for several years in fresh water (see table below) but then comes the spawning urge. They then drop down the rivers, in some cases returning to them through tiny rivulets and brooks, until they reach the mouths of the estuaries. In the process they lose the yellow belly tinge that characterizes older eels and gradually adopt the silver sheen which causes estuary anglers and sea anglers to call them 'silver eels' to distinguish them from conger eels. They remain in coastal waters for some time, while their bodies go through changes enabling them to withstand the pressures of the depths they encounter on their way to and at their spawning area.

Growth rate and the time spent in fresh water vary considerably. By the courtesy of Professor Michael Kennedy and Messrs Hutchinson & Co. I am able to quote, from *The Sea*

Angler's Fishes, the following table and the paragraph which follows it:

'Meek, on the authority of Ehrenbaum and Marakawa, gives the following *average* sizes at successive ages for eels examined by these naturalists.

Age (in years of river life):

	Elvers	1	2	3	4	5	6	7
Length in inches:								
Males	} 2¾	} 3¼	} 4¾	} 5¼	} 7½	9½	12½	14
Females						10¾	13½	15½

'At the time of their metamorphosis into silver eels the male eels have spent from five to ten years in fresh or brackish water, usually six to eight years, and the females from seven to nineteen years, usually ten to twelve years. The upper limits may be considerably extended in individual cases.'

This may seem a long introduction to a fish that many anglers regard as a pest. There are others, however, who set out to catch small and medium-sized eels for the pot, and some who spend hours trying to catch the really big eels that are known to exist. They may catch only a 5- or 6-pounder, but somewhere is the 15-pounder plus!

FISHING FOR EELS

Normally the chance-caught eel is a curse which spoils your bait, causes a disturbance that upsets other fish and leaves you with a slimy bit of well-hooked unpleasantness to deal with.

The techniques for catching the two grades of eels mentioned above – medium and large – can differ considerably and they will be discussed under separate headings, but two subjects common to all eels now follow.

SEASON AND TIMES

Eels normally spend the cold months buried in mud or hidden in bankside holes. When they start hibernation depends, naturally, on the temperature, but also on the type of water. In a canal only 3 ft deep they will feel the effects of cold much earlier than eels in a deep lake in the same temperature area, and eels in deep water are likely to feed long after those in shallow water. Mild spells of weather during the winter may stimulate eels to come out of their haunts to feed, but this applies mainly to shallow water eels where the effects of air temperature are felt almost immediately.

The times of day at which eels can be caught depend in a large measure on their age and size. Small and medium-size eels are caught by the thousand in full daylight, but few large eels – say from 3 lb upwards – are caught before the sun declines, and many have been caught in full darkness. It has been generally admitted that the best time for fishing for the larger eels is between sunset and midnight.

ATTRACTING EELS

Most anglers for coarse fish use groundbait to attract fish to their fishing area. The ordinary types of groundbait for this purpose are not likely to interest eels. I will not go into details, but a long series of experiments convinced me that eels find their food by scent and not by sight. If that principle be accepted, attractor-substances for eels must be specially prepared. There are in the older angling books many strange suggestions for attracting eels, including one of breaking fresh eggs into the water, but eels undoubtedly come to the smell of blood. There are many ways of 'administering' it, I suppose, but the simple method I have found successful over many years is to take an ordinary small round tin, with a lid, and pierce it with holes all round, top and bottom included. Taps with a nail are sufficient. Then fill it with something bloody – liver of any sort is ideal, but any odd bits of bloody meat will do. Fasten the lid tightly with sticky tape. Tie the whole tin to a piece of string, and throw it into the patch you intend to fish. By day or night this device is likely to attract eels. The blood seeps out into the water and eels will gather. They get no substance, but only an appetizer. Any bait in the neighbourhood is likely to be taken.

SMALL AND MEDIUM EELS

This is a short paragraph because the subject is simple. Groundbait as above, and then, with a stiffish rod, 10 lb line,

206

medium-sized hook and a lobworm, start to fish, either with a float or on ledger tackle. No eel in this class is likely to reject a worm and the main problem is waiting patiently for them to arrive instead of moving around in search of them. Once hooked you can pull your eel out unceremoniously and deal with it as described below. If you know the water holds really big eels you can step your line up to 20 lb. The end is attached direct to the hook and the eel will not be disturbed by its diameter.

This tackle and technique is designed for daylight fishing when small or medium-size eels are to be caught. Once dusk falls, larger eels will be on the move, and your line should not be less than 20 lb breaking strain.

LARGE EELS

The big eels normally move out to feed when the light begins to fade. There is too little evidence to enable us to say how long they go on feeding. I have spent several all-night sessions in this pursuit but I have never had the hint of an eel after midnight, nor have many night fishers with whom I have discussed the matter caught eels either immediately after midnight or in the early morning following. One would expect eels, like many other species of freshwater fish, to come on the feed at dawn, but in my experience they do not. On countless mornings in June I have fished for tench in waters alive with eels. As is usual in Spring tench fishing I arrived in the dark and put down my lobworm bait before the first hint of light. No eel ever touched it.

Large eels need stout tackle. There is no question of playing a big eel. It seems to be as happy out of the water as in it, so it cannot be exhausted as can an ordinary fish. It *must* be rushed out of the water and up the bank the moment it has taken the hook. There is no room for finesse. The rod must be strong and almost unyielding and the line strong enough, right down to the hook, to act as a hawser rather than as a fine piece of angling equipment.

The bait should be a small fish. Large lobworms will take large eels, but they will also be taken by ones smaller than those you are seeking. The only way to pick out the size of your eel is to present it with a bait that only a big eel can take. A 2½-to 3-in fish, mounted as shown in Figure 66, is the bait that answers this condition. Sprats have been used with success, but there is no doubt at all that freshly caught freshwater fish have the greater attraction. I have tried many small freshwater fish, but my best catches have been with gudgeon.

Mount at least a dozen on short snoods, so that you do not have to use the same bait twice.

The fishing itself is simple. Having thrown out your tin of blood (or any other attractor you devise) you cast in, sit down and wait. You can cast in the bait on float or ledger tackle. In the dark the float's only use is to support the line, which is not necessary except in weeded water; and the ledger weight is

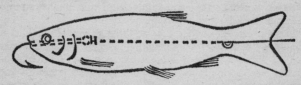

Figure 66 Attach the hook to a gimp or nylon snood and thread into a baiting needle. Pass the needle through the mouth of the fish and out at the tail. Attach a split shot or half-moon lead close to the tail to prevent the bait running up the snood

unnecessary with a fish bait unless you are fishing where the current is likely to move it.

Hold the line. When an eel comes to the bait it will mouth it for some time. Even the largest wide-mouthed female eels cannot swallow a small fish in one gulp, and there will be many twitchings and plucks which must be disregarded. Have plenty of loose line, or disconnect the controls, and wait for a long, firm run, and then again wait for a count of three. Then strike. Strike hard, do not pause, and reel in as quickly as possible, at the same time walking away from the bank and so increasing the speed at which the hooked eel is being drawn in. Once it is on land, do not hesitate to control it. If it is a really big one try to drag it farther inland.

DEALING WITH EELS

If you are out for an ordinary day's coarse fishing and hook an eel the best thing to do is to put your foot on it, cut the hook off and let it slide back. A hook is not worth the bother of twisted tackle and slimy clothes.

When you are deliberately fishing for small or medium eels

the best footwear is *smooth-soled* (as distinct from ribbed-soled) gum boots. These enable you to get your foot on the eel, and the slimy, twisting, tail end will not damage your clothing. Once the head is secured, cut through the backbone immediately behind the head. Then extract your hook or cut off the trace as you prefer.

A useful scheme on a fairly windless day is to have a wad of newspaper in separate sheets. Drop your eel on the top sheet. The paper sticks to the slime and you can handle the eels. Drop it, paper and all, into your container and deal with it at home. The next sheet of paper is ready for your next catch. If there is a strong wind blowing this scheme is more nuisance than it is worth.

For a serious and lengthy eel-fishing expedition I like to have an open-mouthed container hanging vertically from a tripod of three sticks or bamboos. I drop the eel into this and cut off the trace, leaving the hook to be recovered at home when the eels can be dealt with in daylight and at leisure. In earlier years my container was a small sack or sandbag. Now many plastic bags of suitable size are available, for example those in which fertilizers are packed.

APPENDIX I

Coarse Fish of the British Isles: Identification

The following brief descriptions will help you to identify the different species. Colour must only be used as a guide and never as a means of identification if in doubt. Colouring, even in fish of the same species, often varies considerably. This is chiefly due to environment and age.

BARBEL (*Barbus barbus*). Average length: 12–24 ins.

Body rather long and narrow at the back. Snout prominent and lips thick. There are a pair of barbules above the upper lip and one at each corner of the mouth. Colour of back greenish brown, sides lighter brown or yellow. Tail forked and asymmetrical – upper lobe pointed, lower lobe rounded. Fin rays: Dorsal 11, Pectoral 16, Ventral 9–10, Anal 8. Number of scales along lateral line 58–60. Habitat: fast rivers with a bottom of sand or gravel. Feeds on the bottom.

BREAM (BRONZE) (*Abramis brama*). Average length: 12–24 ins.

Very deep body which is compressed behind the ventral fin. Small head. Colour of larger fish bronze with a dark grey or black back. Young fish are silvery and often confused with silver bream. Tail forked. Fin rays: Dorsal 19, Pectoral 16, Anal 24–30, Ventral 10. Number of scales along the lateral line 50–57. Habitat: lakes, ponds and slow-moving rivers. A lover of deep water and a bottom feeder.

BREAM (SILVER) (*Blicca bjoerkna*). Average length: 8–12 ins.

Similar in shape and appearance to the Bronze Bream. Back and top of head dark green, sides silvery. Fin rays: Dorsal 8–9, Pectoral 15–16, Ventral 10, Anal 21–23. Scales along the lateral line 44–48. Habitat: similar to Bronze Bream.

CARP (*Cyprinus carpio*). Average length: 12–24 ins.

Wide variations in shape and type of scaling. The wild form is long and sleek, completely covered with fairly large scales. Selective breeding has produced many different varieties, chief of which are the 'Mirror' carp with a few very large scales and the 'Leather' carp which is almost scaleless. Cultivated specimens, often called 'King' carp, are sometimes completely covered in scales like wild carp, but all, unlike the wild form, are deep bodied and thick, with an amazing capacity for rapid growth. Colour very variable but back usually a bluish grey and sides a golden olive brown. Scales have a metallic lustre and fins often tinged with red. Fin rays: Dorsal 17–22, Pectoral 16–17, Ventral 10–11, Anal 5–8. Scales along the lateral line 35–39. Habitat: ponds, lakes and slow-moving rivers. Carp grow best in warm, shallow weedy lakes which are well sheltered. Chiefly a bottom feeder but often feeds on or near the surface in warm calm weather. The cultivated varieties are more active than the wild form.

CARP (*CRUCIAN*) (*Carassius carassius*). Average length: 6–12 ins.

High-backed and similar in shape to a bream but more compact. Colour generally bronze. This carp is completely covered in scales of medium size and is without barbules. There is a black spot at the base of the tail. Fin rays: Dorsal 14–21, Pectoral 13–14, Ventral 9–11, Anal 6–8. Scales along the lateral line 31–35. Habitat: similar to carp.

CHUB (*Leuciscus cephalus*). Average length: 10–18 ins.

Body long but rather thick set with a large head. Scales fairly large with grey margins. Colour dark green or brown at the top, silver below. Fins often tinged with red. Anal fin convex. Fin rays: Dorsal 8–9, Pectoral 17–18, Ventral 10, Anal 7–9. Scales along the lateral line 44–46. Habitat: chiefly rivers but sometimes lakes. Feeds on the bottom up to the surface depending on the time of year and conditions. Large fish often predatory.

DACE (*Leuciscus leuciscus*). Average length: 6–10 ins.

Similar in shape and colouring to a chub but of a lighter build. Colouring probably more silvery with a steely sheen and dark blue back. Anal fin concave. Fin rays: Dorsal 10–11, Pectoral 17–18, Ventral 10, Anal 10–12. Scales along the lateral line 47–53. Habitat: chiefly rivers and streams, preferring the shallow streamy runs. Occasionally found in still waters. Feeds usually on or near the surface in summer.

EEL (*Anguilla anguilla*). Average length: 12–30 ins.

Snake-like in form and familiar to most of us. Colour dark brownish green above, yellow below. This changes to silver before migration. Habitat: common everywhere in still and moving waters but prefers a bottom of mud. The eel is a migratory fish which spawns far away in the Sargasso Sea. Young eels cross the Atlantic Ocean and ascend our rivers. They frequently travel overland to lakes and pools. The eel is a night feeder taking its food off the bottom.

GUDGEON (*Gobio gobio*). Average length: 3–5 ins.

Similar in shape to that of a barbel. Colour, grey or greenish brown on back and upper sides, golden below with a reddish tinge. A series of black spots along the lateral line. Unlike the barbel possesses only one pair of barbules, one at each angle of the mouth. Fin rays: Dorsal 5–7, Pectoral 15–16, Ventral 10, Anal 6–7. Scales along the lateral line 40–44. Habitat: prefers running water with a gravel bottom but will live and flourish in certain lakes and ponds. A bottom feeder.

PERCH (*Perca fluviatilis*). Average length: 6–12 ins.

A predatory fish with a broad high body, small head and large eyes. There are two dorsal fins, the first of which is large with prickly spines and has a black spot at the rear end. Colour of back and upper sides greyish green changing to green tinged with gold below. At least six vertical black stripes on sides of the fish which is covered with rough scales. Fin rays: Dorsal (1) 13–17, Dorsal (2) 13–16, Pectoral 14, Ventral 6, Anal 8–10. Scales along the lateral line 58–68. Habitat: common practically everywhere.

PIKE (*Esox lucius*). Average length: 12–36 ins.

Body very long, head long and flat with a very large mouth, eyes large. Colour: greenish brown on upper parts becoming lighter on the sides and mottled. Fins often tinged with red. Fin rays: Dorsal 19–23, Pectoral 14, Ventral 9, Anal 16–21. Scales along the lateral line 105–130. Habitat: rivers, lakes and ponds, usually in quiet water away from the main stream. A predatory fish.

PIKE-PERCH, European (Stizostedion lucioperca). Also Zander or Sander. Average length: 16–20 ins.

A predatory fish with slim rounded body, mouth with wide gape and numerous small teeth interspersed with canines. Colour of back and sides, green to blue-grey: underside, matt silver. Black spots on dorsal fins. Tail slightly forked. Fins: Dorsal (1) 13–17 spines (2) 1 or 2 spines, 19–24 rays. Pectoral, 15. Ventral, 1 spine, 5 rays. Anal, 2–3 spines, 11–12 rays. Scales on lateral line: 80–95.

PIKE-PERCH, American (Stizostedion vitreum). Called the Walleye in North America. Average length: 16–20 ins.

Similar in general shape and teeth formation to the foregoing. Colour of back and sides, olive green. White spots on dark background on second dorsal and tail fins. Fins: Dorsal (1) 17–18 spines (2) 20–22 rays. Anal: 2 spines, 12–13 rays. Scales on lateral line, 80–89.

ROACH (Rutilus rutilus). Average length: 6–12 ins.

Rather deep body, particularly in larger fish from still waters; smaller specimens and river fish more streamlined. Silvery in appearance with a bluish green back and red fins. Position of dorsal fin immediately above or only slightly behind front of ventral. Fin rays: Dorsal 9–11, Pectoral 16, Ventral 10, Anal 9–11. Scales along lateral line 42–45. Habitat: common practically everywhere but prefers rivers of medium flow. Feeds on or near the bottom but often near the surface in warm weather (see Figure 67).

RUDD (Scardinius erythrophthalmus). Average length: 6–12 ins.

Deep body. Colour similar to that of a roach but rather more striking. The silver of the body is often tinged with bronze or

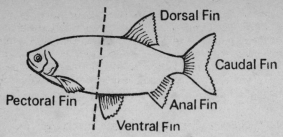

Rudd. Anal fin, 13–15 rays. Dorsal fin, 10–12 rays. Pectoral fin, 15–16 rays. Ventral fin, 9–10 rays. Caudal fin, 17 rays

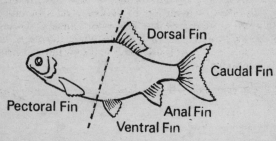

A true roach. Dorsal fin opposite ventral. Anal fin, 9–11 rays. Dorsal fin, 9–11 rays. Pectoral fin, 16 rays. Ventral fin, 9–10 rays. Caudal fin, 19 rays

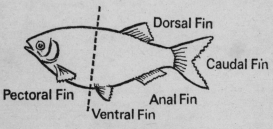

A roach-bream hybrid

Figure 67 Distinguishing marks

gold and the fins, particularly the lower ones, are a brilliant scarlet. The beginning of the dorsal fin is conspicuously behind the root of the ventral. Fin rays: Dorsal 8–9, Pectoral 16–17, Ventral 10, Anal 10–11. Scales along the lateral line 40–43. Habitat: warm shallow lakes and sluggish rivers. A surface or near surface feeder; occasionally on the bottom (see Figure 67).

TENCH (*Tinca tinca*). Average length: 10–18 ins.

Body thick and powerful, fins rounded but tail sub-truncated. Scales are very small and there are two barbules, one at each angle of the mouth. Colour: usually a pure olive green in young fish changing with age to various shades of brown, greyish green or golden bronze. Fin rays: Dorsal 8, Pectoral 16–18, Ventral 10–11, Anal 6–8. Scales along the lateral line 95–100. Habitat: shallow lakes, ponds and slow moving rivers. Chiefly a bottom feeder.

ZANDER, or SANDER, see PIKE-PERCH, European.

APPENDIX II

River Authorities
England and Wales

The Avon and Dorset River Authority: Rostherne, 3 St Stephen's Road, Bournemouth, Hants.

Bristol Avon River Authority: Green Park Road, Bath, Somerset.

Cornwall River Authority: St Johns, Western Road, Launceston, Cornwall.

Cumberland River Authority: 256 London Road, Carlisle, Cumberland.

Dee and Clwyd River Authority: 2 Vicar's Lane, Chester.

Devon River Authority: County Hall, Topsham Road, Exeter.

East Suffolk and Norfolk River Authority: The Cedars, Albemarle Road, Norwich.

Essex River Authority: Springfield Road, Chelmsford, Essex.

Glamorgan River Authority: Tremains House, Coychurch Road, Bridgend, Glamorgan.

Great Ouse River Authority: Great Ouse House, Clarendon Road, Cambridge.

Gwynedd River Authority: Highfield, Caernarvon.

Hampshire River Authority: The Castle, Winchester.

Kent River Authority: River House, London Road, Maidstone.

Lancashire River Authority: 48 West Cliff, Preston, PR1 8NP.

Lee Conservancy Catchment Board: Brettenham House, Lancaster Place, London, WC2.

Lincolnshire River Authority: 50 Wide Bargate, Boston, Lincs.

Mersey and Weaver River Authority: Liverpool Road, Great Sankey, Warrington, Lancs.

Northumbrian River Authority: Dunira, Osborne Road, Newcastle-upon-Tyne, 2.

Severn River Authority: Portland House, Church Street, Great Malvern, Worcs.

Somerset River Authority: The Watergate, West Quay, Bridgwater, Somerset.

South West Wales River Authority: Penyfal House, Llanelli, Carmarthenshire.

Sussex River Authority: Anston House, 137–139 Preston Road, Brighton, 6.

Thames Conservancy: Burdett House, 15 Buckingham Street, London, WC2.

Trent River Authority: 206 Derby Road, Nottingham.

Usk River Authority: The Croft, Goldcroft Common, Caerleon, Monmouthshire.

Welland and Nene River Authority: North Street, Oundle, Northants.

Wye River Authority: 4 St John Street, Hereford.

Yorkshire Ouse and Hull River Authority: 21 Park Square, Leeds 1.

APPENDIX III

Knots

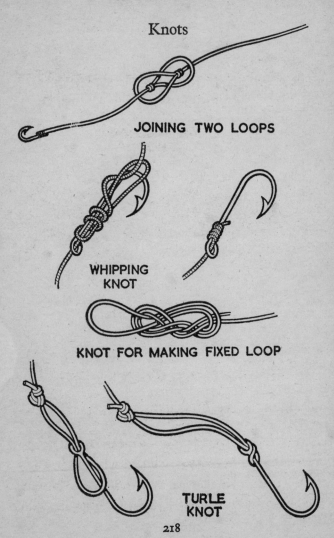

JOINING TWO LOOPS

WHIPPING
KNOT

KNOT FOR MAKING FIXED LOOP

TURLE
KNOT

DOUBLE BLOOD KNOT

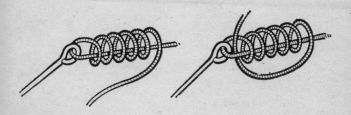

HALF BLOOD KNOT

Whipping knot. This forms a secure knot for eyed hooks, as shown, but it can also be used for attaching spade-end (blind) hooks. There is no eye through which the nylon can be passed, but a length is held straight along the shank, and the end brought back to form the loop. The rest is as illustrated.

Turle knot. A knot for attaching cast to hook. It is generally used for attaching artificial flies.

Double blood knot. A knot for joining two lengths of nylon of roughly similar diameter.

Half blood knot. The knot now in general use for attaching hooks, swivels, etc.

Index